75¢

AN   641.59716 GIL   C.3
Gill, Janice Murray, 1934-
Nova Scotia down-home cooking /   MBA

3 3281 00068 0022

W9-DIN-524

ed from Inventory
ph Public Library

GUELPH PUBLIC LIBRARY

X

1979

641.5
9716
GIL
C.3

Gill, Janice Murray
     Nova Scotia down-home cooking by
Janice Murray Hill.   Toronto:
McGraw-Hill Ryerson, 1978.
     208 p.

Please do not
     Includes index.
remove Cards
     1. Cookery, Canadian - Nova Scotia.
I. Title.
0-07-082777-X   C78-001269-0

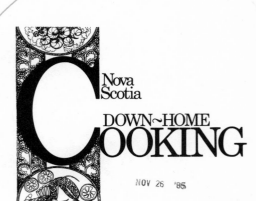

Nova
Scotia

DOWN~HOME
COOKING

NOV 26 '85

Nova Scotia DOWN~HOME COOKING

BY JANICE MURRAY GILL

McGRAW-HILL RYERSON LIMITED

Toronto	Montreal	New York	St. Louis	San Francisco
Auckland	Beirut	Bogotá	Düsseldorf	Johannesburg	Lisbon
London	Lucerne	Madrid	Mexico	New Delhi	Panama
Paris	San Juan	São Paulo	Singapore	Sydney	Tokyo

14.95

10/8/79

GUELPH PUBLIC LIBRARY

641.59716
GIL
C.3.

Nova Scotia Down-Home Cooking

Copyright © Janice Murray Gill, 1978.

All rights reserved. No part of this publication
may be reproduced, stored in a retrieval system,
or transmitted in any form or by any means,
electronic, mechanical, photocopying, recording,
or otherwise, without the prior written permission
of McGraw-Hill Ryerson Limited.

ISBN 0-07-082777-X

1 2 3 4 5 6 7 8 9 10 D 7 6 5 4 3 2 1 0 9 8

Printed and bound in Canada

Canadian Cataloguing in Publication Data

Gill, Janice Murray, date

Nova Scotia down-home cooking
Includes index.

ISBN 0-07-082777-X

1. Cookery, Canadian — Nova Scotia.* I. Title.

TX715.G55   641.5'9716   C78-001269-0

To my mother, Elsie Bond Murray

Contents

Introduction

In rural Nova Scotia during the thirties and forties, geography, economics, and finally the war, all combined to limit our resources in all things, from cultural to culinary. In many ways this was a great advantage, for, if we had little, we learned to use what we had to best advantage. This was particularly true in the case of food. While we lived for the most part on what was produced in the region with a few staple imports, we lived very well indeed. Now, with unlimited imports of delicacies from the ends of the earth, we have an exciting variety in our diet but all too often the quality is not of the best. One reason for this is that as far as the supermarket is concerned the seasons have almost disappeared, and urban dwellers, at any rate, have forgotten when any particular product is "in season" and consequently at its best. This is not only true of fresh produce; there are certain types of meals which taste better at particular times of the year, and in the format of this book I have tried to recall not only what we ate but when we ate it and how good it all was.

All the recipes in this book are old. Some took many hours of careful preparation and were abandoned when premixed and commercially prepared substitutes became available. Today, however, with a renewed interest in home preparation from basic ingredients and with the help of the wonderful new appliances currently available, there is again a place for these recipes. I have not "updated" them by suggesting "short cuts" or substituting premixed ingredients, but where an appliance will do a chopping, mixing, churning, or slow cooking job, it makes sense to use it. What I have done to bring these recipes into the seventies is to supply metric alternates. I use the term "metric alternates" instead of metric equivalents deliberately, for the metric amounts given are not the equals of the Imperial measurements; instead, they are the amounts which I have found the easiest and most convenient to use and which give the best results for any given recipe. Therefore, a cup of flour in one recipe may have a metric alternate of 250 mL, while in another a cup of cream may have an alternate of 200 mL because that is the volume of the containers in which cream is sold. I hope that other cooks will use this book as a handy guide for switching their own treasured family recipes into the new, easy, and efficient system of measurement.

Whichever system is used, I hope that the recipes will prove useful and that you will share with me the "good eats" that we used to have "down home."

Metrication

Metrication is about to enter the life of every Canadian cook — and high time! Though there may be a few initial difficulties, at the end we will be working in a far easier and more sensible system. It is my hope that this book will help its users over the hump of transition.

First of all, what does one need to "go metric"? Not very much and none of it expensive: two sets of standard metric cup and spoon measures (if one set is in steel it will cost a little more but you can put it on the stove to heat small quantities), a large pyrex litre measure divided into a 25 mL scale (don't get one with an Imperial scale on the other side, it will only lead to confusion), and finally, a good kitchen scale calibrated in grams and kilograms (some are calibrated in both systems and unlike the two-system measuring cup this can be very useful, especially if you have any British cookbooks which you wish to convert). This then, is all you need and you are ready to switch.

Why is it necessary to switch? Why can't one buy a lifetime supply of Imperial measuring cups and carry on in the old way? This sounds feasible but really, as more and more ingredients are sold in metric units and books and magazines publish their recipes in metric, life will become very confusing for the cook who is trying to work with two systems. Imagine trying out a new cake recipe using metric measures and then making the filling with an old recipe; how easy to pick up the wrong measure and spoil everything. No! The answer is to change over once and for all and put away the old measures in the back of the cupboard where they may one day emerge as valuable antiques.

With new recipes written in metric there is no apparent problem at first. The cook is told to take the new cups and spoons and get to work, measuring and levelling as one always did. What could complicate that? Nothing except the fact that the user may find it difficult to decide whether or not to make the item in the first place, for, with the unfamiliar values it is hard to "read" a recipe and know what the finished product will be like. The answer to this is that one must change already familiar recipes into metric terms, and in this way get used to the lock of a list of ingredients with big numbers like 25, 100, and 250 instead of fractions and small, whole numbers. Here is where this book comes in. Side by side, you see the two sets of measurements and, at first, you can check the old measurements to see just how rich a pastry is or how big a pudding, and then you can go on to work with the new ones. Soon you will not need the old ones at all.

You can also use the same system as I did to change the values in your own cookbooks. No cook could spare the time for the infinitesimal gradations of amounts necessary if Imperial volumes were translated into precise metric equivalents. Instead, a table can be used to substitute one for the other. It is important to remember that all baking is simply a matter of proportions: 1 part sugar, 2 parts butter, 3 parts flour, and 1/48 part baking powder, which can be written 1 cup sugar, 2 cups butter, 3 cups flour, and 1 tsp baking powder; OR it can read, 250 mL sugar, 480 mL butter, 720 mL flour, and 5 mL baking powder. All you need to do is decide what ONE Imperial ingredient will be in metric; then put all the OTHER ingredients into metric, keeping them in the same proportion to the first ingredient as they were in the Imperial recipe.

Let us take an example from the book. On page 141 is the recipe for Spotty Dog. Since all the ingredients are in equal proportions, we simply take the most convenient measure in metric (in this case the 250 mL measure), and use 250 mL of each ingredient; the proportions remain the same.

Generally speaking, this is what we do when translating: we say, "Let 1 cup be equivalent to 250 mL." Then, ½ cup will become 125 mL, and 2 cups will become 500 mL. Since 1 tbsp is 1/16 of a cup, it will become 1/16 of 250 mL which is 15.62 mL. Now, it's not really possible to measure as exactly as that. Also, 15.62 mL, expressed another way, is 15 mL plus ⅔ of 1 mL. If you look at a 1 mL measuring spoon, you will see that ⅔ of it is a negligible amount. Therefore, we can call 15.62 mL simply 15 mL rounded, meaning a spoonful that is *very slightly* heaped. Since 1 tsp is ⅓ of 1 tbsp it then becomes 5 mL. While I used these alternates for most of the recipes in this book, there are a few exceptions. Sometimes, there are recipes which call for many ⅓ or ¼ proportions. Then I found it was easier to use 240 mL as the alternate for 1 cup as it was evenly divisible by 3 and 4. Finally, since eggs are not going to change their size when you go metric, I found, in the few recipes where the eggs were the only source of liquid, that it was necessary to keep the dry ingredients in proportion to them and therefore it was necessary to use exact equivalents. In these cases, I let 1 cup become 225 mL. Doing this also gave a batter that was almost exactly the same volume, which was important in the case of some baking vessels. After all was done and all the recipes tested, I found that the system "boiled down" to the following table:

		A	B	C
WHEN 1 cup	becomes	**250 mL**	**240 mL**	**225 mL**
THEN ¾ cup	becomes	185 mL	180 mL	170 mL scant
⅔ cup		165 mL	160 mL	150 mL
½ cup		125 mL	120 mL	112 mL
⅓ cup		82 mL	80 mL	75 mL
¼ cup		65 mL	60 mL	55 mL rounded
1 tbsp		15 mL rounded	15 mL	14 mL
1 tsp		5 mL	5 mL	5 mL scant
½ tsp		2 mL rounded	2 mL	2 mL
¼ tsp		1 mL rounded	1 mL	1 mL
1 medium egg		1 extra-large egg	1 large egg	1 medium egg

Use column A for most recipes; B for recipes where there are many ⅓ and ¼ cup proportions; and C for recipes where exact equivalents are required.

Since manufacturers have not yet started producing ovens with Celsius thermometers I have not given oven temperatures in the system. However, when they do come in, this simple conversion table is straightforward.

F°	C°	
250	130	cool
275	140	warm
300	150	
325	165	moderate
350	180	
375	190	
400	200	hot
425	215	
450	230	very hot
475	240	

PART 1

Dining Down Home

January

THE NEW YEAR began with a feast. This was as it should have been, for we ate superlatively well all year round and the great New Year's dinner was a fitting introduction to another year of gourmandizing. Our Scots background determined the importance of this holiday and, if we did not partake of the bibulous delights of Hogmanay, on the New Year's day itself the transplanted Caledonians sat down to a meal very similar to a New Year's dinner in the "auld sod." Goose was the bird. Now, it is very difficult to be sure that a goose will be tender, particularly if it is a large one and the phrase "tough but tasty" might have been originated to describe a large percentage of roast geese. My mother had licked the problem and her geese invariably turned out tender and succulent; and for flavour the goose is the king of domestic poultry, incomparably better than the ubiquitous turkey. In turning out this annual miracle, my mother confessed that she was aided by a superb roasting pan which she had got from her mother-in-law. At one time, having a gargantuan bird which would not fit any pan she owned, mother went to my grandmother and asked if she had a large roaster to lend. From the depths of the farthest scullery cupboard my grandmother dug out an enormous double roasting pan. Made of blackened, sheet steel it browned beautifully with the lid on. Mother used it, and when she came to return it, full of praise for its merits, my grandmother told her she had better keep it for she herself hated it. The reason for this prejudice was the fact that my grandfather had given it to her as a present and, outraged at so utilitarian a gift, Mama Murray had refused to use it. I suppose that my grandfather learned his lesson and there-after put a little more romance into his offerings; but the roasting pan carried on and every time it was used his descendants blessed him.

The goose would, of course, be stuffed with potato dressing for bread dressing soaks up too much of the fat; but in addition to the dressing would be oatmeal puddings or marrigan. These are sausage casings stuffed with a mixture of oatmeal, onions, and suet, and then boiled. They are then stored and reheated before serving. The nutty flavour is incredibly delicious especially served with poultry. Since the goose was stuffed with potato there would be no plain potatoes served as vegetables; instead potato mashed together with turnip to make "clapshot," buttered parsnips, bottled green beans, and pickled beets would be heaped up on the plates. A huge bowl of mother's russet applesauce would complete the course. Many people seem to use russet apples only for eating but the applesauce made with them has a pleasant spicy flavour and they need little sweetening. There was also the inevitable "red jelly" which always seemed to accompany any meat. This was usually red currant or crab apple but might also be rowanberry made from the fruit of the mountain ash.

After all this there was dessert. For those with iron stomachs, mince pie was of course available; but for anyone whose digestion and spirit of tradition were weaker, mother always had a Bavarian cream with candied fruit.

The day after New Year's was my birthday and a very poor time for it too I have always thought. I imagine that faced with a children's party immediately after Christmas and New Year my mother must have agreed with me but she never complained. Birthday parties then were extremely simple but utterly stylized. Everyone wore the same sort of dress, gave the same sort of present, served the same sort of food, and played the same sort of games. There was no nonsense with favours, loot bags, pony rides, or conjurors. The party was held in the parlor in winter, in the garden in summer. We went after school; birthdays were always held on the actual day unless it happened to be a Sunday. This was a good idea as it limited the time. We all wore our good dresses and hair ribbons. Ribbons were very important articles of dress. All of us had boxes of them — satin, taffeta, plaid, woven with flowers — one to match every dress. I had some nice ones; but one girl had a collection of ribbons that seared our souls with envy. She had received them from an aunt who lived in India. Brushed and beribboned, we played Farmer in the Dell, Musical Chairs, and In and Out the Window if we were indoors; and Giant Steps, Paddle in the Duck's Water, and Hoist the Green Sail, if we were out. At suppertime we were called in to the dining room and the presents were opened. We had a supper which was always sandwiches: chicken, egg, and peanut butter; and then ice cream and cake. The ice cream was invariably strawberry, but the cakes differed. Mine was a pound cake and, inspired by pictures of the movie stars' wedding cakes in *Life* magazine I insisted on having two tiers. One tier was always white, the other pink, and they were covered with lots of boiled icing. The icing appealed to the taste of children, but mother's pound cake was fit for the gods. It was light, with a fine flavour and a soft texture like velvet. My best friend always had a chocolate birthday cake and I have never tasted a better one. The secret in making good chocolate cake is always to use all butter. The butter flavour enhances that of the chocolate.

School started again right after my birthday. The walk to school was not long but it was cold for I had to cross the bridge and the wind whistled in off the bay and went right through you. Elderly people used to tell us that, in the old days, wooden sides were put up on the bridge to cut the wind; but that had been in the time when we were a busy town with thriving shipyards. How I regretted that the practice had been discontinued, as I walked crab-wise over the bridge, my back to the wind.

The river itself would be frozen solid and on Sundays people could take their cars out on the ice. Again, we would be told of the horse-and-cutter races on the ice but I can only remember seeing one. When the ice was solid, the fishermen used to set their smelt nets between two poles pushed down through the ice into the bottom of the river. These beautiful little silver fish with golden brown undercolour were delicious when simply prepared: heads removed, bodies cleaned, shaken in cornmeal, and fried in butter. The colder the water a fish is taken from, the better the flavour and texture. These little fellows swimming around under the ice certainly had a delicacy out of all proportion to their size.

In winter the horse came into his own. Though many people had cars and trucks, in the winter the danger of getting stuck was too great and out came the horse and sleigh. My father, unwilling to trust the Chrysler or even the little Ford on the back roads, kept a horse in the winter. Trixie, a little bay mare, took my father, well wrapped in his ankle length raccoon coat, with his charcoal burning footwarmer, over miles of country roads on his sick calls. All the mail drivers used horses too, and drove about in little wooden houses set on runners, equipped with a stove whose tin chimney stuck out of the roof. The reins went in through holes in the front and the driver peered out through a slit window above them. Eight or ten of these rigs used to stand outside the post office every morning waiting to collect the mail for the rural delivery.

To fortify themselves for the rounds, the drivers had probably consumed the same sort of breakfast as was given to me before I set out for school — almost every man, woman, and child in the village was expected to consume a large plate of porridge every morning. This was usually "real" porridge, made with oatmeal rather than newfangled quickies like creamed wheat or rolled oats. Porridge made with oatmeal takes a long time to cook and my mother usually made it the night before, leaving it on the back of the stove to be warmed up in the morning. Real porridge is well worth the effort, for its nutty flavour and creamy texture are quite unlike the "library paste" porridge that results from instant or five-minute brands. When oatmeal porridge cools it solidifies, and my grandmother used to slice leftover porridge, warm it up in butter in a frying pan and serve it with molasses. If my mother had not made oatmeal and needed a quick hot cereal, she sometimes made use of Pablum. Since my father had his own drugstore he always had large stocks of Pablum on hand, and she could go into the office and help herself to one of the huge round cardboard boxes in which Pablum was sold at that time. She used it a lot in cooking and had a repertoire of recipes enriched with this, for her, handy ingredient. Puddings, muffins, date squares and bread — she had Pablum recipes for all of them. Oatmeal was also used in baking of this type. In our kitchen were three large bins, each holding fifty pounds and these were filled with flour, sugar, and oatmeal. The oatmeal was used to make oatcakes which might be either thick and sweetened, or thin, crisp, and dry. They were buttered and eaten instead of bread. I never knew of anyone using oatmeal to make real Scottish haggis boiled in a sheep's stomach, but pot haggis was a simpler variation, boiled in a pudding basin. Its rich, savory goodness was wonderfully filling. It is the best way I know to get children to eat liver and love it. Mother would serve it on January 25th to mark Burns's birthday, but I fear the bard would have found little cheer at our board as no dram accompanied it.

The attitude toward liquor in our village was uncompromising — all or nothing. If you were a respectable pillar of any one of our four churches you never touched the stuff. If you were a miserable, backsliding sinner you got full every time you had the chance. Actually, most of the people who claimed to be teetotalers really were, although the damning whisper, "He drinks you know!" did circulate about some of them. In any case, the civilized glass of sherry before dinner, the carafe of wine with dinner, or the tot of brandy afterwards were not possible. Spirits were seldom used in cooking either, although Christmas was an exception and the medicinal brandy bottle might be brought out to liven up the fruit cake. This had certainly not always been the case and, in fact, our own house had originally been built as an inn, and a lively trade had been carried on in the taproom there. However, I have found that the excellent food I enjoyed in those days is equally good whether accompanied by wine or not; and where wine or spirits are indicated in the recipes, it is always optional for they were not used in the originals.

Every day that it was possible during the month of January we went skating. We had no rink but the frozen river, and that was really safe for only about two months. Even then you often got a bit wet because the river, being tidal there, always had unfrozen water at the edge during high tide and one had to find an ice bridge to cross over this moat. Once out on the river proper you could skate for miles although much of the ice was rough and washboarded and we tended to stay in sheltered spots where the lack of wind had let the ice freeze smooth and "glib." Often, we would take baked potatoes in our pockets to keep our hands warm, eating them when they had cooled. At least once a season, the boys would go around to the service stations and collect old tires. A pile of these on the ice made a gorgeous bonfire, as long as you stayed up wind of it, and the banks of the river were high enough to keep the smoke away from the houses. We would skate till the flames died down and then go home for huge mugs of cocoa, real cocoa made with top milk. Top milk is the milk from the top of the bottle, for, in those unhomogenized days, each quart of milk from MacDonald's good Jersey cows wore a golden head of cream that came halfway down the bottle. Poured off, this cream was used for tea, porridge, and for making that incredibly wonderful and rich cocoa. If for some reason you ordered cream, you got a pint of concentrated richness, too thick to pour.

RECIPES — JANUARY

February

THROUGHOUT THE SCHOOL YEAR, the beginning of each new month was marked by the teacher's attaching to one of the side blackboards a tissue paper stencil, which we then belaboured with well-chalked felt erasers. When the stencil was stripped off, there was a new calendar for the month with spaces for chalking in symbols to record the weather. February's calendar would be wreathed with hearts and flowers. It is easy to see how St. Valentine survived the reformation when all of his holy associates, with the exception of St. Nicholas, received short shrift from the iconoclastic Puritans. After all, even a dissenter could not remove the only bit of light from the terrible bleakness of February. For us children, Valentine's day came just after Hallowe'en in importance. It wasn't a holiday; it was almost better — a school day in which we did no work, the morning being devoted to preparing for the Valentine party, the afternoon to having it. An elaborate Valentine box was decorated and stuffed with the Valentines on which we had spent all our spare time for the past week. At the party, after the cards were distributed, we had a lunch, each child having brought a contribution. Mother always gave me a special Valentine cake which I carried proudly in a special, flat cake basket. There was no Tupperware then, but the Micmac Indians made beautiful woven baskets for every conceivable purpose, and came around selling them. In the red, green, and purple dyed basket the great white cake used to look magnificent. It was light and moist with a rich buttery flavour. Mother iced it with Italian meringue into which she folded cut up maraschino cherries. Another item I remember from these Valentine parties was the sugar cookie. Someone was always sure to bring these, sweet and crisp, two heart-shaped cookies sandwiched together with strawberry or raspberry jam.

For those young people who were past the age for school Valentine parties, one of the church groups or lodges would hold a box social. This was a particularly appropriate form of entertainment to honour the patron saint of lovers, for the local swains were required to put their money where their mouths were, and pay for the privilege of their girlfriends' company. The slightness of many a young man's regard was demonstrated when he refused to cough up sufficient cash to pay for the box lunch the lady had brought to be auctioned. By the time I was old enough to go to box socials, such functions had ceased. Perhaps it was just as well; I might have had to endure the terrible shame of having a box unsold, or worse, bought by a kindly relative. I do remember spending the day with a friend whose older sister was preparing for one of these affairs. "Remember, if George asks what my box is like you can tell him — but only if he asks, mind! If Don asks, don't you dare let on. I'd rather eat with Dad than him!" The point of these lunchboxes was that they contained a lunch for two, and the producer ate with the purchaser. The food inside was supposed to be prepared by the lady herself; and it usually was. Most girls began cooking at about age nine, and could feed a family of six or eight by the time they were in their teens. The lunches they took to box socials were designed to show off their culinary skill to the utmost. The meat was usually chicken, and at that time of year the "chicken" was most often a superannuated laying hen which required very careful cooking indeed if it were to be neither tough nor tasteless. When properly handled, fowl is extremely good and I am sure that no young man who ate one of these birds was put off by the fact that his inamorata had commenced the preparation of the delectable feast by wielding the chopper and beheading the bird with her own fair hands. The chicken would be accompanied by rolls — always soft — for strangely enough, I don't remember anyone making crusty ones. There would be potato salad made when the potatoes were hot, for then the salad looks better, keeps longer, and is not as soggy as when cold boiled potatoes are used. There would be a great selection of pickles to round off the first part of the meal, followed by cake or pie — or even cake *and* pie, with a few cookies or "squares" to fill up the corners. After he got through all this, if he could still walk, the buyer could take the girl home. I suppose, today, exponents of women's liberation would be horrified at the implications of the box social. However, in our community and others like it they did no harm to the female self-image. As soon as she was aware that she was female, the girl of that place and time *knew* that she was a superior and fortunate individual. All around us, we saw examples to prove that what women said — went! The wealthiest and most influential person in the place was a woman. She had the biggest house, best car, and most say in the village. She had a husband too, but he was regarded rather in the same light as Albert, the Prince Consort. In fact, I rather think his name *was* Albert. Our four churches were run by the women; true, each one had a male clergyman as a reverend figurehead, but except for a sort of perfunctory respect for his "cloth" none of the women paid him any mind.

The village merchants were men, of course, but everybody knew that they were "run" by their wives, and if my father, the doctor, had some authority, it was strictly limited to the medical field. As for the farmers' wives, with their own little businesses of hens or market gardens, they often had more real cash money than their husbands, and in any case their equal contribution to the daily running of the farm was too valuable for their husbands to try any male chauvinism with them. Girls of the village knew that they were the ones who would probably finish school, go to college, train for nurses, or go to Normal School and become teachers. They could then go away if they wished and earn their living, while their brothers stood a far greater chance of quitting school, and spending the rest of their lives in low paid, semi-skilled work. In these circumstances who wouldn't be a girl? Armed with this firm feeling of superiority, the girls quite happily learned to cook and sew and I very much doubt if any of them ever felt trapped by a male chauvinist. If they did they knew how to deal with him.

For me, as a child, February had one other big day. On the evening of the third Thursday of that month, the Missionary Meeting was held at our house. The ladies whose homes boasted furnaces always hostessed the winter meetings and, falling into that category, my mother drew February as her month. In later years three other ladies brought the lunch, but when I was very young the hostess did it all. All the best teacups and serving plates were brought out. Silver was polished, so were floors. I took the ladies up to the spare room to "lay off" their coats and hats and, while the business and devotions meetings were held, stayed upstairs and tried them all on. After this I went down to help serve the lunch. There were the usual sandwiches, but the number and variety of the sweets was what counted. Perhaps there were women who were diet conscious back then but I can recall no evidence of it. Mother always made a beautiful little butter cookie she called a Dutch dainty. She also had an apricot "square" that appeared on this occasion. These were two perennials but there were others that varied from year to year. Everyone said her coconut macaroons were good, but I hated coconut and still do so I have never tried them. Quite different were the cookies my friends and I were served after school, or perhaps after a straw ride when one of the farmers would fill up a big pung with straw, hitch up his team and take the church young people's group for a sleigh ride. Ravenous after this, we would go to someone's home and be given huge, hot, molasses cookies, great round gingersnaps, and jam tarts. The chocolate chip cookie of today pales into insignificance beside those mouth-filling, chewy wonders.

Now that I think back, February really was a very social month because, of course, there was less farm work to be done and no fishing, though some men did work in the woods. Everybody went to the weekly card parties where the game invariably was auction 45s, a game known to all Maritimers and inexplicable to anyone else. Since a hand consists of only five cards, the game goes quite quickly; and moving tables after each game, one could spend some time with almost every person in the village before the evening was over. For those who didn't play cards, there were prayer meetings, Ladies Aid meetings and Oddfellows' and Rebeckahs' Lodges. And there was always a lunch. The importance of sweets at this time of year lay in the fact that they imparted greater variety to the diet since there was not so much fresh fish or meat as at other times. Of course, there was beef, but we used less pork, and lamb was out of the question. Veal was rarely eaten, mainly, I think, because farmers disliked killing a healthy calf. Salt or "pickled" pork we did have, but in the late months of the winter most housewives relied on their baking skills to keep the meals interesting — and they always succeeded.

RECIPES — FEBRUARY

March

IN MARCH, the ice in the river grew grey and rotten, gradually breaking up into large cakes which afforded the boys an exciting annual sport — jumping ice cakes. A game of tag was played from one side of the river to the other, leaping from floe to floe and occasionally getting tipped into the icy water. Even if total immersion was avoided, everyone got wet to the knees. Of course it was strictly forbidden, but all the boys did it during the few spring days that the ice drifted in and out with the tide. Dangerous though it appeared, generations of boys tested their agility and audacity and no one was ever drowned. The breakup of the ice and the melting of the snow brought sugaring off time. Though Nova Scotia does not produce the great volume of maple syrup that Ontario and Quebec do, its syrup is of excellent quality. Possibly this is because the relatively small amounts made by most farmers are intended primarily for their own use. Before she was married, my mother had taught school in a small district called Mapleton. It was from there that we used to get gallons of the most wonderful maple syrup. Maple cream we got as well, great slabs of it looking like Sunlight soap and tasting like heaven. Many things are said to "melt in the mouth," but when I hear the phrase I think of biting off a big square of maple candy. It was the arrival of the maple syrup, rather than Shrove Tuesday, that set off the orgy of pan-cake making at our house. Mother made regular ones, but she also made a beautifully light, yeast-raised buckwheat cake. The batter for these was mixed the night before and the cakes were fried in the morning. Regular pancakes were as likely to be eaten for the evening meal as for breakfast, a habit of which I approve for then one can eat more of them. Maple syrup meant more than just pancakes though. Every woman in the village had her own special recipe using syrup, and there were maple buns, maple cookies, maple cake, and maple custard. The maple-sugar pie, so loved in Quebec, was not made, as far as I know, but it was a great time for steamed puddings smothered in the syrup as a sauce. The simplest of these was spotty dog, but carrot pudding and applesauce pudding also could be served with maple syrup.

In days gone by, among the ships built in our village were some with names such as "Banshee" and "Faughaballagh"; but, in spite of this indication to the contrary, there were few people of Irish background living there, so St. Patrick's day was little remarked. Sometimes though, "just for fun," my mother would make corned beef and cabbage on that day. It is quite simple to corn beef at home; one needs only a large crock, and the product is far superior to the plastic-coated supermarket brisket. With the corned beef and cabbage there would be boiled potatoes as well as carrots, turnips, onions, and "doughboys," mother's lighter-than-air steamed dumplings. The relish with which we demolished a huge platter of this dinner proved that everyone is a little Irish on Paddy's day, even in Pictou County.

For me, March was the month when my grandmother came home, if she had spent the winter in Montreal as she sometimes did. This was a great day, for in her trunk would be a number of beautiful new dresses, just for me. My grandmother was a superb needlewoman, and occupied almost all her spare time sewing and knitting for her eight grandchildren. Her homecoming also meant that I could spend much of my time at her house, for she was alone and none of her other grandchildren lived in the village. Her kitchen was a second home to me. It was an enormous, L-shaped room, easily able to accommodate a large table, a sofa, a rocking chair, my grandfather's great, old, black leather armchair, a book case, a sink, and a pump with a big wooden handle to pump drinking water. The electric pump only handled the soft rainwater collected in a big brick tank. All these pieces of furniture seemed somewhat insignificant, however, for the room was dominated by the biggest, blackest, shiniest cooking stove I have ever seen outside of a hotel or restaurant kitchen. When the stove that had been installed in 1900, when the house was built, finally burned out, my grandmother, her family grown up, cherished dreams of a new, up-to-date, white enamel stove. My grandfather with his customary attitude of "nothing but the best" scorned the products of local, Maritime foundries and ordered the stove from the firm in Montreal who had supplied the original. It turned out that they had ceased producing stoves for domestic use, building them only for the commercial market; however, they agreed to build one to my grandfather's specifications. What my grandmother thought when she beheld the nickle-trimmed, black, iron behemoth she never told; but, unlike the roasting pan, she couldn't refuse to use the range and, once in use, it proved to be a matchless cooker and baker. The bread that came out of its oven was, of all breads, the best. Most of the women in the village made their own bread, and all of it was good; but two bakers made bread of outstanding quality. One was my grandmother; the other was Vida Stramberg, a wonderful cook who, at ninety-five, was able to tell me how she did it, for she made that wonderful bread still. That bread tasted best spread with marmalade. Vida made wonderful marmalade, too, with the California oranges and lemons that were always available; but, once in a while, the stores would have a few cases of the little, bitter Seville oranges, and then, my grandmother would make real "Scottish" marmalade, with a bittersweet tang and a richer colour. My mother had a store of little, stone crocks in which she sealed her marmalade, and to spoon it out of one of these enhanced the already superb flavour.

In March, the spring had advanced far enough so that the danger of snowstorms was pretty well past; but the farmers could not yet get out on the land. Since people still had some spare time, it was a good season to hold some functions for making money for the various churches. Therefore, March was the month of church suppers and the Rebeckahs' sale. The church suppers were usually either chicken or ham suppers with the invariable dessert of pie. Ham, as we knew it, was not much like the waterlogged, ready-to-eat stuff most people today regard as ham. Hard and black, the hams had to be scrubbed with soap, water, and a stiff brush before they were boiled for a long, long time. When they were finished, though, they had a magnificent flavour. At the suppers, they were usually served with scalloped potatoes, baked tender and crusty. At home, we had stovies instead, potatoes thinly sliced as if for scallop; but instead of being baked, they were simmered gently on the back of the stove. The back of the stove — what a useful place, not to be found on the four-burner electric or gas range! The new, smooth-top cookers are not so new. The old, wood-and-coal range had a smooth top — about twelve square feet of it, giving the cook infinite gradations of heat, from the searing flames when a pot was set directly over the fire where a stove lid was removed, to the gentle warmth at the back of the stove, where a stockpot could be kept simmering for weeks. Nowadays, my stockpot lives in the freezer, and is brought out and boiled up as I need it; but the stock is not the same.

That stockpot provided the basis for all our homemade soups. The stock itself was strong enough to make a good consommé with nothing else added; but as soup was expected to suffice for the main course when it was served, it had to be "hearty." Soup rarely tasted the same two times running, for no housewife in her right mind bought a list of ingredients just for soup; she used up what she had on hand. There were a few soups that were distinctive, although the ingredients varied widely from day to day. One was scotch broth, for the thickening was always barley though the broth might be beef or mutton. Vegetable soup always contained onion, turnip, and parsnips and whatever else that might be added, as did the chicken soup which was made from the boiling fowls. Pea soup was made with ham bones; and cullenskink was the wonderful Scots name for a milk-based soup made with finnan haddie.

I mentioned earlier the pies which would be produced for the community suppers. While all the village women made good bread, there was not the same uniformity in their pastry making; and it was on the quality of her pies that a cook was often judged. When you attended a church supper, you passed a table full of pies as you went to your seat — usually at a long trestle, with ten or twelve people to a side. Having a chance to look the pies over beforehand made you better able to make a wise decision when the waitress asked what kind you wanted. In March, there would not be any fresh-fruit pies, or their imitations made from a freezer; but there was still plenty of choice — apple (not too many by this time of year), lemon, raisin, custard, coconut cream, or apricot. My grandmother made a very good raisin pie, made more tart by the addition of cranberries.

The Rebeckahs' sale was truly a community affair, for the lodges were the only social groups that cut across the sectarian lines laid down by our four churches. It was a mammoth affair, originally instituted to raise money to pay for the Oddfellows' hall that had been burned in one of the fires that periodically swept the community. Until after the war, these fires were fought by the local men with a small gasoline pump and bucket brigades. A fire always provided great excitement, and I felt in the thick of things for the fire "engine" lived in our barn. I remember being told stories of how Charlie Hines sat astride the ridge pole of a burning building, pouring buckets of water through a hole chopped in the roof; and ducking back to avoid the flames shooting through, until his hair and eyebrows were singed off. Another fire story I often heard was how the shop across from my grandfather's drugstore was burning, and my grandfather was watching the progress of the fire, which had been brought under control. A man ran past with two buckets of water, no longer needed and, anxious not to waste his effort, he flung the water at the front of the drugstore, whose paint was blistering with the heat. Helpless, my grandfather watched the cold water hit the big, plate glass window — his pride and joy, now too hot to touch. At home, we had a nice glass tabletop made from a piece of that window.

RECIPES — MARCH

April

Late in April, with the spring truly arrived, the owner of the general store at the corner of the bridge would mix up a thick paste of "Bon Ami" and use it to paint across his window in large white letters: FRESH MACKEREL. Mackerel, a streamlined, tiger-striped, glossy, silver-blue fish should never be eaten away from the coast. The flesh is dark and quite oily, and its flavour changes very quickly after it is caught. Mackerel can grow to quite a size but we always chose to eat the little tinkers, plate-sized mackerel, to be prepared fried, soused, or stuffed and baked, at 25 cents a piece — a combination of flavour and economy hard to match.

The store where the fish were bought was one of three general stores in the village, all similar in layout and stock. To the left as you entered was a long oak counter with groceries stacked on, behind, and under it. To the right was its twin, piled with dry goods, from bolts of flannelette and muslin, to Bearcat exercise books and fish hooks. At the end of the aisle between them stood the iron-hooped, wooden puncheon, fitted with a cast-iron pump, from whose spout always hung a drop of dark-brown molasses. This was the basis for the delicious molasses cookies our mothers produced by the ton. When you wanted to buy some molasses, you took your own quart bottle and had it filled at the store. Kids loved this chore, for you always got a few free licks at the end. Behind the barrel was the meat room, a blindingly clean little cubicle, scrubbed out daily by the owner's aged aunt, who never set foot outside the door but spent her life in maintaining a Dutch standard of cleanliness on any surface she could find to scrub. Making a series of sick calls on the living quarters above the store, my father took to calling earlier and earlier in the day, hoping to catch a glimpse of her. Invariably, the steps were freshly washed but she was gone. Finally, one day he achieved success in that he saw the tail of her skirt. Invisible she may have been; but, thanks to her, it was a pleasure to stand in that sunny cubicle, with its window over-hanging the river. Perhaps it was the salty air blowing in which seasoned the meat into that "tasty bite" of sirloin steak that the owner would cut for us. And he always tucked a free piece of liver into the package for my cat!

Throughout the week, but especially on Saturday night — "open night" — these stores served as community meeting places; but they also had a second and more serious social function. Many, many families through the hard years of the Depression ran up large bills for the necessities of life; and no one, in those hard times, ever had more understanding or patient creditors. I remember once hearing a person who was paying for a very large order say jokingly, "Don't I get a discount for paying cash?" The owner's wife responded with complete seriousness, "Oh no! It's the cash customers that we live on." No one will ever know the thousands of dollars in unofficial welfare donated to the unfortunate by storekeepers like these, in contrast to the often painted picture of the grasping merchants who exploited poor fishermen.

When the worst of the mud was over on the roads, we usually got a visit from the School Inspector. This was always great fun, for it was his habit to visit all four rooms in turn, and demonstrate to the teachers how to teach a lesson. The teachers changed, and often the lessons were new to them; but they were not new to us, and we quickly gave the required answers when asked. Everyone enjoyed their part in this little drama; and we were re-warded for our participation since the Inspector always told the teacher to dismiss us for the rest of the day when his visits were over. The school nurse also made the rounds in the spring. She looked through our heads to see if we had lice; and everybody watched carefully to see if anyone got a note to carry home. If she looked for anything else I have no recollection of it, but in any case we were a pretty healthy crowd, spending most of our time out of doors.

Easter came; and, with it, a visit from my beloved Aunt Chris who would bring me a basket filled with eggs and chocolate rabbits from the stores in town. Easter dinner might be lamb if Easter was late enough; but this was unlikely, and it was usual to have ham. The dozens of eggs that I had blown the week before, in order to decorate the shells, were utilized to make a beautiful, rich butter cake — layered with red jelly and frosted with yellow butter cream — which mother called "daffodil cake." The top was decorated with lines of dark chocolate studded with blobs of white icing to represent pussy willows. We also had pans of hot cross buns, soft, warm and spicy; but I was usually too full of the Easter Bunny's (Aunt Chris's) chocolate to eat very many. One year, there was to be a dance on Easter Monday at the Oddfellows' hall, and mother had been asked to make a cake for the food sale at the end of the evening. She allowed me to make the cake, and so successful was I and so lavishly did I decorate it, that they decided to auction it off so as to raise more money from it. What a triumph for me! Who would buy this gorgeous confection and realize the full scope of my culinary skill? To my utter chagrin, the buyer was a funny little bachelor who lived all alone in the woods up at the Branch, emerging only for dances, where he had considerable ability as a caller. His presence caused consternation among the girls, for you could not refuse to dance if asked, and this gentleman always left the imprint of his undeniably grubby paw on the back of a lady's dress. My mother thought it was lovely that the poor old soul got the nice cake; but I felt that my efforts to impress had been wasted.

Toward the end of April, the ground had dried out sufficiently for the business of "getting in the garden" to commence. In our family, my father prepared the soil and helped with the planting, and mother did the rest. I hated gardening, and always contrived to get out of doing any work at all, although I certainly was not backward when it came to eating the delicious produce. Our garden was behind the garage where our property sloped down to the river, so the drainage was good; and as it faced south, vegetables and fruit ripened early. The four corners of the garden were marked out by fruit trees, two apple, a greengage and a damson plum. Inside this space, my father would lay out beds of such geometric precision, filled with such beautifully raked earth that it looked gorgeous even before anything grew in it. Down at the bottom was an asparagus patch, and, there, asparagus tips would already be starting to show, beside the bright, pink knobs of the rhubarb crowns. Over a couple of the latter buckets would be placed, acting as forcing covers. In the dark, the rhubarb would shoot up and, very early, be ready for pies while the other crowns would be left to come on more slowly. Next, there was a cold frame, made from an old storm window, into which would be set the little tomato seedlings. Walking up the garden, you came to a double row of potatoes, red-jacketed ones, and above them again were set up the stakes supporting chicken wire, where the peas would be planted. Next, came the long poles for the beans to twine around; and, finally, a bed of carrots, one of beets, and a couple of rows of lettuce. Up near the house, parsley, chives, and dill grew among the flowering plants, and mint grew around the stone coping of the well. When one stood there to draw up a bucket of water, the aroma of the bruised mint leaves filled the air and made the water taste even better.

When the garden was "in" it was the result of quite a few hours of hard work; but no one who has not had access to freshly gathered, homegrown produce can know the true sweetness of peas in the pod, the tenderness of tiny new potatoes, or the delicacy of baby beets. Not only do the market vegetables lack something in freshness, but flavour is not the prime consideration for the grower. Often, the best-tasting varieties are only available as seeds; and many of the varieties known thirty years ago are not now obtainable anywhere — a great loss to the gardener.

More will be said about the preparation of these vegetables as the summer progressed; but at the end of April, weather permitting, the newly-planted garden was merely the substance of things hoped for, and we turned our minds to the next great event of the year — May 1st and the OPENING OF THE LOBSTER SEASON!!!

RECIPES — APRIL

May

EARLY, EARLY IN THE MORNING, on the first day of May, I would awaken to the noise of the boat engines. All the lobster boats would start out, top-heavy with gear, to lay their traps in their chosen spots in the Northumberland Strait for the short (two-month), lobster season. The lobster boat is a graceful vessel, usually a Cape Island, about 40 feet long with a high flaring bow. Powered by gasoline engines — often taken from a car — the boats cruise out to where the traps are set. A lobster trap's resting place on the sea bottom is marked by a distinctively painted wooden buoy. This buoy is attached to a length of string which, in turn, is attached to the trap. The lobster trap is a simple structure of wooden slats, built over a hooped frame in the shape of a half cylinder. The double bottom is filled with flat beach stones as ballast, and the main part of the trap is divided into two chambers by a net with a funnel shaped opening in it. The lobster crawls into the first chamber through a hole on top, and through the funnel into the baited inner chamber; but, because of the shape of the opening, he cannot get back and must wait there until the trap is lifted. The fisherman removes the lobster by unhooking a door in the side of the trap. If the lobster is too small, or a berried (egg-carrying) female, it is thrown back; but, if it is marketable, wooden pegs are quickly driven into the claws to keep them shut. Then the lobster is thrown with his mates into a heavy, lidded, wooden fish box. When all the traps are lifted, emptied, rebaited, and reset, the fisherman turns his boat for home and brings his catch to the wharf. Most of the lobsters go direct to the "factory" to be canned or frozen; but some are brought home and sold, either live or freshly boiled. We would hear a boat come in, and a short time later a little plume of smoke from the stovepipe sticking out of Jim Thompson's fish shack would tell us that lobster would be ready for supper. Mother would give me $2 and I would trot down the road to bring home all the lobster that the three of us could eat. The process is still the same but for $2 I would not get much more than the smell of the pot! We served our lobster in the simplest way possible. The freshly boiled lobster was drained and cooled; the meat was removed from the shell and served, seasoned with salt, pepper, and a few drops of vinegar, with potato salad. If the meat was eaten hot, then the pieces were dipped in clarified butter. There is really no trick to opening a lobster, but long practice can bring an impressive speed. The crackers who work at the factory can get all the meat out of a lobster in a few seconds. The most efficient way is to use a pair of lobster cutters and a long pick. First, remove the two big claws and all the small walking legs. Then split the tail off from the body. The body is filled with a greenish liver called tomalley which is considered, by some, to be a delicacy, but it should be kept separate from the white meat of the lobster. The two big claws are broken off from the arm; the meat from them can be extracted in one piece, if a heavy knife is placed just above the joint and tapped with a mallet. This will crack the shell so it can be split in two and the claw meat will drop out. The lobster cutters are used to cut open the shell of the arms and tail, and the meat is removed. Last of all, the feathery gills are cut off the ends of the little legs and these are lined up and run under a rolling pin, squeezing out little tubes of tender meat. Although dressing up a lobster is truly "gilding refined gold," sometimes we had to do it when, for some reason, the lobster meat had to be "stretched." Then, my mother made lobster salad and, since she garnished each serving with a whole claw, this was almost as good as the whole lobster. Nowadays, this type of salad is served at the "lobster suppers" that are put on as a means of raising money for the local churches, but years ago people were too busy at that time of year, and the lobster suppers were not begun until the fifties. These often featured lobster "stew," which wasn't really a stew at all but a milk-based chowder, a soup of truly demoralizing deliciousness. As my mother used to say, "It doesn't matter how much you make, they will eat it all." One other way in which we partook of lobster was as a picnic or lunchtime snack, in the form of a lobster roll — all the meat of a small lobster cut up, mixed with a little salad dressing, and piled on a soft, chewy bun shaped like a hot dog roll. For some reason, the salad dressing used by the village women was always a boiled dressing; I do not recall ever having either the classic mayonnaise or a French dressing. Why this should have been I cannot understand; but it was a pity, and proved one of the few deficiencies in the repertoire of our village cooks.

As the weather grew warmer and warmer, we school children began to pester the teacher to take us on a nature walk; and finally, one warm and sunny day, she would succumb — doubtless, because she herself could not bear to be inside on such a perfect afternoon. We would walk up the hill toward the station and then follow the track for a little way before striking off into the fields to look for Mayflowers. The Mayflower (trailing arbutus), is the provincial flower of Nova Scotia and is, perhaps, the most beautiful, if the least showy, of all Canadian wild flowers. Crawling over the ground, the woody stems bear small, leathery leaves and an efflorescence of small, star-shaped, pink-and-white flowers. We picked them in huge bunches like cabbages; and, although the delicate beauty of the tiny flowers was lost, the scent from one of the bouquets was ravishing. The Mayflower has one of the most beautiful of all floral fragrances, and is one of the few that does not remind me of a funeral parlour. Besides Mayflowers, we would look for something else on our nature walk; namely, fiddleheads, the tightly curled tips of the bracken fern. Fiddleheads are usually thought of as a New Brunswick dish; but Nova Scotia has them too and, if we found some, we filled a paper bag, brought for the purpose, with these delicacies, the very first of the "spring greens." Any recipe for asparagus can be used for fiddleheads, but they are best when not overcooked.

There were other greens that could be found growing wild, much nearer home. These were dandelion greens and pigweed. Both had to be picked very early, for bad weeds grow fast and in just a few days their tender shoots would be sturdy plants, amazingly woody with long taproots that made it impossible to pull them. From the dandelion, we picked the young perfect leaves, unmarred by insects; and from the pigweed, a close relative of spinach and beet, we gathered the "tassels." These tassels were the tender leaves which grew at the tip of each plant, just before the spot where the plant started to branch out. Mother made a delicious "weed soup" from the pigweed. This, I think, was the early Scots settlers' substitute for the sorrel soup of the old country, which is also known as Mary, Queen of Scots Soup; and I am sure that mother's weed soup was equally fit for a Queen.

It would be about this time of year that my father would take to carrying his fishing rod in the car with him, and arranging his calls to end up, late on a warm spring afternoon, near one of the brooks that flowed down from the hills behind the village. He would come home with enough small, speckled trout for a meal. Our trout were never very big — 6 to 8 ounces were keepers, and a 10 to 12 ounce trout was a leviathan — but were they good! Later, as the water got warmer, they would acquire an earthy taste; but early in spring, while the pools were deep and cold and the water fast, these little fish were perfect for panfrying. Many people try to fry trout that are too big, and then the flesh becomes dry; only the smallest should be panfried, and the pan should be of the traditional heavy, cast-iron type. The meal was perfect when mother refried sliced, cooked potatoes, and served these with the trout and a serving of fiddleheads. For dessert, there would be the first of the rhubarb, baked in a lattice-topped pie or in a deep dish with a crumb crust. Either was perfect to follow the fish.

The last week of May was marked by two special days for most of the children of the village. Queen Victoria's birthday was still a holiday and still called the Queen's birthday, for everyone was still tremendously anglo-phile and royalist. This holiday gave us a carefree day; but, for those of us who trudged once a week to the house on the outskirts of the village where the local music teacher lived, there was the prospect of another day — the day of the McGill conservatory exam when the "professor" from far-away Montreal would come to test us. Our music teacher had tremendous dedication and an amazingly modern approach to the teaching of piano to children. We put on musical plays, and made elaborate scrapbooks com-bining musical theory with nature and fairy stories; but we also spent hours working on the "pieces" for the exam. The train schedule meant that the distinguished visitor would have to be accommodated overnight, and he always stayed at our house. All my co-students declared that I was secretly coached the night before the exam. In fact, so concerned was my mother that he might hear me play accidentally, that the piano was locked until after I had taken my test.

My mother felt that, after the arduous task of listening to twenty-five or thirty children playing the same pieces over and over again, the poor man was entitled to a good dinner; and she laid herself out to provide one. Lobster stew to begin with, accompanied by the crustiest of rolls; then, the tiniest and most delicately flavoured lamb chops from the very first of the spring lambs. With these, would be asparagus tips and browned rice, for, by now, the potatoes were very old and not good enough to "go with" such delicate fare. For dessert, mother might bring in a beautiful vanilla soufflé. I know now that what we called a soufflé was not a true soufflé but rather a soufflé pudding. Although it is not quite as high-rising as a French-style soufflé it is more dependable and has the advantage that it will repuff if it is heated over the next day. For a sauce, we might have strawberry preserves or mother's astonishingly simple and good chocolate sauce. So May would finish and it would be summer.

RECIPES — MAY

June

SCHOOL CONTINUED throughout most of the month of June but, with the exception of those high school students who were preparing for the provincial exams, most of us took it pretty easy. The "bad" boys played hookey, and the "good" boys turned up in body but were absent in mind. We played endless games of ball in the field across from the school, often luring the teacher out to play with us. The windowsills of the classrooms were crowded with jars of pollywogs, and the teacher's desk was hidden under a drift of lilacs, torn from my aunt's big bush that overhung the fence into the schoolyard. Underneath the windows at the front of the school, the big, old damask rose bushes would be covered with pink blossoms; and with each puff of breeze from the river their strong fragrance would permeate the room to blend with that of the lilacs.

June was the month of roses then, for few people had begun to cultivate the hybrid teas with their long blooming season. Instead, nearly every garden in the village had a Harrison's Yellow — a 6 foot fountain of golden blossoms — and perhaps a little Scotch rose, covered with tiny pink blooms the size of an acorn in the midst of fern-like foliage. A few gardens had an American Beauty with its magnificent red flowers. The roadsides were lined with single pink "wild" roses that had escaped from some pioneer's garden. The petals of this rose could be candied and so could the young buds. Many a June wedding cake was decorated with the sugar-frosted roses, and was much more appealing than the sculptured products of the town bakers. At the wedding reception, there would always be two cakes. The bride's cake, the tall, tiered one, would be a plain pound cake; and the groom's cake would be a large, square fruitcake, less elaborately iced than the bride's. Each guest would be served a piece of each, and the plates of cake would be carried round by the bride and groom themselves, a pleasant and friendly custom.

For the newlyweds, a slightly less pleasant custom was the "tinpanning," although no real harm was meant. When the couple returned from their honeymoon, it was the custom for all the children (and some of the adults) of the village to surround the house and make a fiendish din with bells, horns, washboards, tubs, and anything else that would make a noise. They would continue until the groom came out and paid them to go away. When this was done promptly, a good time was had by all; but, occasionally, strangers who didn't understand the custom drove the young children off. Then the older ones took this as a licence to commit acts of vandalism that eventually destroyed what had been a quite harmless custom.

June was the month of the salmon run. In streams throughout the province, the Atlantic salmon came home to spawn. Unlike their Pacific cousins, these salmon did not then die but instead returned to the sea. Besides the salmon, there were the sea trout — brook trout that "go to sea" for a period of time. These ran twice, once in May and again in late June; the later run seemed to produce the most fish in our area. With them came the gaspereaux, and the shad or "poor man's salmon." The gasperaux were too bony for good eating but the shad were a delicious meal. They were members of the herring family, and schools of them might be seen "boiling" just beneath the surface of the stream.

Now all of these fish were "game fish" and were sought by some fishermen with appropriate tackle; but other fishermen considered them "fair game" and pursued the salmon, in the short June nights, with a bright flaming torch and a big, two-pronged spear. This was certainly more efficient, if less sporting! It was also reprehensible, no doubt, and we never dared look a gift salmon in the mouth lest we should find that he had not been hooked! What did we do with these gorgeous fish? Well, the sea trout were generally cooked whole, and large cuts of salmon were prepared in the same way; that is, poached in a court bouillon. The fish could then be served either hot or cold. The salmon might be cut into "steaks"; but these were not broiled, and I think this was just as well. Too often, have I been served pieces of dried-up, pinkish felt — the result of overbroiling salmon. When mother got salmon steaks, they were individually wrapped in well-buttered paper and baked. This kept the juices where they belonged, inside the fish. The herring could, of course, be fried; but at our house we were more apt to treat it in the south shore fashion and pickle it to make solomon gundy.

The settlers of Lunenburg County were sturdy German subjects of George III, brought out to farm and to feed the new city of Halifax. Finding it impossible to farm the solid ironstone of Nova Scotia's south shore, they turned instead to the sea, and became the first and greatest of our fishermen, sailors, and shipbuilders. Their German words and accent lingered in their speech, becoming somewhat corrupted by their Yankee neighbours. Solomon gundy is an instance of this for it was originally salmagundi; but however you spell or pronounce it, it is an excellent way to prepare herring.

As an appetizer or a snack it can't be beaten, and since it keeps for months we always had it on hand. With a fresh tomato, a few leaves of lettuce, and cucumber slices, it made a satisfying lunch.

The shad could be poached too; but, since its flavour is a bit more assertive, we more often had it baked, or mother might panfry the fillets. The usual size for baking was about 4 pounds, and if mother was going to stuff it, as I always begged her to, then it was my job first to remove as many bones as possible.

I have mentioned before that sophisticated sauces were not in my mother's repertoire; but the simple ones that she and her friends made were always perfectly done and without that gluey, pasty consistency that characterizes the efforts of many an amateur saucier, armed with a French "gourmet" cookbook, a lightweight saucepan, and a small store of patience. With our fish we had "white" sauce with a beautifully light and delicate creaminess that brought out the flavour of the fish. This sauce was simple, but it took both patience and concentration, together with a good heavy pan.

As June days grew longer and longer with sunset holding off until late in the evening and the light lasting until after ten o'clock, it grew harder and harder to stay in school; but, at last, the day came when we went to school with a present for the teacher, and saw the pile of buff-coloured envelopes on the desk. These were the report cards and for some, at least, their appearance was menacing. The teacher took the last roll call; we emptied our desks, took down the pictures, the Junior Red Cross posters, and the progress charts. At 10:30 a.m. the bell rang for recess and we were dismissed, each one getting his or her report card as he shook hands with the teacher and said good-bye.

The theory behind this method of dismissal was that the student could go out to the hall and look at the report card without anyone peering over his shoulder; but, as all the pupils who had gotten out earlier waited outside the door, the cries of "Did you pass?" greeted each one who emerged. All the way home, every adult you met would also ask, "Did you pass?" while occasionally an elderly person would phrase the question in the old-fashioned way — "Were you a good scholar?" These questions were quite serious for there was no automatic promotion from one grade to the next. Children could, and did, spend several years in the same grade, the dullest remaining in the lower grades until their sixteenth birthday provided a merciful release from a school desk long outgrown. The fact that our school had three grades to each room made it a little easier for the majority of those who failed a grade; and a determined effort the following year often enabled a student who had slipped to "catch up."

Still, there were often tears on that last day of school, even among those who had passed. The girls would often be weeping buckets at the prospect of saying "good-bye" to a beloved teacher; but, by the time we got home, the crying would be over and it would be a golden day, the first of an endless succession of summer holidays. Mother would always have some special thing for lunch that day — perhaps for dessert some Washington pie, which I loved.

The warm weather was, of course, the time for ice cream; but in those freezerless days we had to buy the ice cream in the summer for there was nowhere to store the ice needed to make the homemade variety. One year, there was an exception. The man next door was tearing down an old house; and on the blazing June day that he finally took up the floor boards we found a huge pack of ice, insulated there since the winter. His daughter and I immediately determined to utilize this Antarctica to make ice cream and tore in, demanding that mother drop whatever it was that she was doing and help us. She good-naturedly agreed (my father loved ice cream), and started making the custard while Jean and I chopped ice and cleaned the churn. That was the best ice cream I ever tasted. Unfortunately, however, I didn't get much, because we decided to become businesswomen and sell our ice cream at the roadside. We quickly disposed of our stock; but the next morning, when we decided to repeat our business success, we found that overnight all that great big cake of ice had melted away and we were without the means to replenish our stock. Vastly disappointed, we split the profits of the previous day's sales and walked across the village — to buy some ice cream.

The end of the school year was always coupled with the end of the Sunday school year, which was climaxed by a picnic. Everybody who had gone to Sunday school faithfully all year went to the picnic. Everybody who had started to go to Sunday school at the beginning of June, in anticipation of the picnic, went also! We had races — foot, spoon, and sack varieties, and the minister took off his coat but kept on his clerical collar and judged the contestants. The refreshments were pretty unremarkable, except for the lemonade which was the standard beverage. One woman used to make it and her method produced gallons of wonderful-tasting lemonade, as far removed from the ersatz packet product as vintage champagne is from fizzy pop. This day was a real celebration for us and so, quite unknowingly, our little village church followed the early Christian tradition of scheduling a church celebration on the occasion of pagan festivities, and we too satisfied desires for merrymaking with a festival at the midsummer solstice.

RECIPES — JUNE

July

In July, after the two hectic months of the lobster fishing season, the fishermen took a couple of days off to celebrate; and the celebration became the lobster carnival. Nowadays, this carnival and the others like it — the Annapolis Apple Blossom Festival and the various Highland games held throughout the province — seem to have become chiefly tourist attractions; and certainly a great many people from "away" come, enjoy themselves, and spend money. Everybody has a good time, but there is a little less of the "family feeling" that there was in the years just before, and after, the war. Then, the condition of our roads was such that almost all of our summer visitors were expatriate Nova Scotians, home for the holidays; and their presence at these gatherings only added to the sense of intimacy.

Our lobster carnival was held in Pictou and was a genuine "free" show. All the attractions were open to everyone without paying a fee. The big feature was the parade. It went along Water Street which was crisscrossed with strings of signal flags; every streetlight carried a lobster trap converted into a hanging flower basket. The fishermen marched in the parade together with kilted Highland pipers, and floats from the fishing villages and local businesses. Maritimes Packers and Ferguson's would draw "oohs" and "aahs" for their large elaborate entries; but the biggest hand would always be reserved for the inevitable small boy in cap and overalls pulling his express wagon on which rode a 12 or 14 pound live lobster. Occasionally, the lobster would decide to get off and the parade would be held up while he was persuaded to remount his chariot; but nobody minded — the parade was never on time anyhow. Pictou has never been a place where split-second timing is important, and it has the effect of slowing down visitors as well. So powerful is this that even royalty, with their proverbial punctuality, are affected; and on the only two State visits to Pictou in my lifetime, royalty have been late.

 GUELPH PUBLIC LIBRARY

The carnival day always continued with boat races in the harbour; and when people got hungry they could go to the Lobster Garden, pick their own lobster, and watch it being boiled. At night, the harbour was gay with lights, while people square danced in the streets to the tune of old-time fiddles — maybe even Don Messer and his Islanders over from Charlottetown for the great day. The fireworks ended the day, climaxed by the apparition of the Phantom Ship of the Northumberland Strait, ghosting up the harbour and bursting into a blaze of fire and rockets. Then we would head for home; and I would be sound asleep in the back seat before we even left the paved streets of the town to drive the 20 dusty miles back over the Old Post Road to the village and home.

July seemed to have one great day after another, for soon my aunts would come home, bringing their families with them from the big cities of New York and Montreal. Before the great gifts of Drs. Salk and Sabin, summer was a worrying time for mothers in large cities; everyone who could got her children away to the country, where the danger of polio was less. We children were unaware of this grim reason for our summers together; we only knew that it was summer and Nova Scotia in summer is a grand place for kids.

My grandmother's big quiet house became a summer resort hotel as three families with seven children among them descended upon it. My grandmother got a cow who took up her summer residence in the field behind the house and, as I seem to recall, gave straight cream when my grandmother milked her. There were some hens too and, since they seemed to lay their eggs whenever and wherever it occurred to them, my cousin Diana and I spent a lot of time looking for eggs, while being careful not to disturb the cow who was somewhat neurotic and "took after" us whenever we got too close.

How we ate in those glorious summer days! My mother, my grandmother, and my aunts all seemed to spend a great deal of time preparing the meals to fill us all up. The lamb would be at its best, the animals weighing about 30 to 35 pounds; and, according to some people, mother's boned and stuffed leg of lamb tasted even better served cold than it did served hot.

What mother could do with a leg of lamb! First she boned it; and the bone and shank wouldn't be wasted either — they went with the neck to make a soup so thick with the new vegetables just coming out of the garden that it could hardly be called soup. We called it jumble. The boned leg would be stuffed with bread dressing, sewn up, and roasted. Was it better served hot or cold? We never could decide! The loin of lamb was cut into chops, and these were panbroiled in the big, heavy, cast-iron pan. All lamb was served with the new potatoes and peas, brought in from the garden only an hour before we ate them. The mint jelly would be mother's own; and there would be red currant jelly as well, for the currants would be ripening. The breast of the lamb was stuffed with the forcemeat made from the trimmings and some of the shoulder meat, while the rest of the shoulder went into chops. Not a bit of the lamb was wasted, for the head made sheep's head broth; and a fearsome thing it was to lift the lid of the big kettle and see the severed head glaring at one like Medusa. Frightening though it was, it never put me off the broth.

The bones served as the basis for the scotch broth made with the fresh vegetables appearing daily in the garden. One of the most appetizing meals to come from the garden at this time of year was hodgepodge — an almost meatless dish that combined all the fresh vegetables in turn, each at their peak of perfection. It varied slightly from week to week, but each variation was better than the last.

As the weather grew hotter and hotter, we spent more and more time in the water. When we went swimming there was no elaborate paraphernalia of beachwear or water toys. The girls were encumbered with an old towel and a bathing suit; but the boys (when alone) even dispensed with that. On our shore, the water is relatively shallow and heats up as the tide creeps in over the hot sand. Our beach was free of undertow, and we spent hours in water that at times reached 75°. No wonder Nova Scotians are sometimes suspected of having webbed feet. On coming home, we would be ravenously hungry but the salt water would also have given us a raging thirst; this we quenched with gallons of lime juice, the most refreshing of all summer drinks. I suppose the taste for lime juice originated with the sailors who, of course, had it on board ship; but it had long become a fixture ashore. Everyone — from the haymakers sweating in the fields to ladies relaxing on the garden swings or porch gliders — drank glasses of the beverage. The juice was bottled under the name Monserrat and, as a child, I always pictured that island as a huge lime orchard whose total production was consumed by Nova Scotians. My mother had another tried-and-true thirst quencher which she made herself — root beer. The Hires Company, besides selling the bottled variety, also produced the extract which could be used at home to make a drink much superior to their bottled product. It was a little stronger-flavoured and contained less sugar. It also was somewhat more powerful than the commercial variety since the CO_2 was produced by fermentation; if a bottle got overlooked and was left too long, it could go off like a cannon. Once mother gave my grandmother a bottle and she, having I suspect, a distrust of any beverage called beer, no matter how innocuous, put it away and did not use it. Long afterward, I found it and insisted on its being opened. Opened it was, as soon as grandma touched the cap; and although the house had 9 foot ceilings, the brown stain on the one in the pantry proved the height of the root beer fountain. I watched in delighted horror, convinced that it was a judgment on anyone who neglected to drink root beer as soon as it was ready. I remember another delicious drink from that time, though my mother did not make it; namely, raspberry vinegar. This was offered to "callers" on summer evenings, and seemed to go with the creak of porch gliders as people "sat out" and watched the spectacular sunsets.

When the weather was fine, great numbers of people, both adults and children went picking berries and gallons were brought home to be "put up" for the winter. The strawberries came first and my mother was an indefatigable picker. One year, I remember, 40 pints of wild strawberry preserves went into her jam cupboard. What hours of patient picking that represented. We children always referred to cultivated strawberries as "tame" berries. This was an apt term for them because there was just that difference in flavour, the cultivated berry being bland without the wild tang. We always preserved all of our wild strawberries, for that was how their superiority of flavour showed to best advantage. For table use, the "tame" ones, freshly picked, were very good indeed, especially with the thick yellow cream from Mama Murray's neurotic cow, or in strawberry shortcake made with one of Big Aunt Jean's perfect biscuits. "Big" Aunt Jean was my great aunt and was so called to distinguish her from "Little" Aunt Jean who was my father's sister. The adjectives had nothing to do with the ladies' relative sizes, as both were on the small side. Big Aunt Jean had no children of her own so she became a universal aunt to the whole village. On summer evenings, her porch, or "piazza" as she called it, would hold a crowd whose ages were from 7 to 70, all having a grand time. She loved people, and she loved travel, and she had something in common with every person she ever met. Like all my female relatives, she could cook, but her baking powder biscuits were the thing she made best. They were snow white and feather light, with a perfection of shape as if turned out of a mold. Split one of these, fill it with sliced strawberries, and cover it with cream — bliss. She made other kinds of biscuits as well, oatmeal biscuits, whole wheat biscuits, etc. It didn't matter what kind they were; all were absolutely perfect.

As soon as the strawberries were finished, the raspberries ripened; and while picking strawberries in a sunny, open hayfield was a pleasure, wild raspberry picking in the woods was a hot, scratchy, prickly penance. Even mother was less enthusiastic and, frankly, I hated it. Nevertheless, mother insisted on going after them, and brought home basketfuls to be made into rich, ruby jelly. They were too seedy for jam — that came from the home-grown variety and even these were a nuisance to pick. If they were being served fresh, they had to be carefully looked over for worms. My grandfather always refused to eat them because he said people didn't clean them carefully enough; one day he took a dish and carefully selected his own berries, examining each for traces of occupants. In triumph, he came in and proceeded to sugar his raspberries; but, alas, just as he was pouring the cream, out came a little white worm. "Dammit," he raged, "the things are MADE of worms!" In fact, raspberries can very easily be cleaned if they are immersed for a minute or two in salted water. All the residents come out and the berries are quite clean. They also make a wonderful pie.

As we picked our berries, overhead the birds were after the cherries and it was a race with the robins to get the makings for the best of all fruit pies — fresh cherry pie, even better than raspberry. No canned or frozen cherry can give a pie with the same flavour. The pitting is a lot of work; but oh! Is it worth it! I watched the tree anxiously for days, hoping that the birds would leave enough. They always did; but the adults' gloomy prognostications that "the birds will get them all this year," kept me in agonies of apprehension. The birds always left enough for some jam as well, and the delicious juice from cherry preserves was used as a wonderful dessert sauce all winter.

The beautiful July days would follow each other, each bringing some new addition to our store of summer plenty. But, gradually, the greens would become more golden, and the evenings a little more purple; and then it would be August.

RECIPES — JULY

August

Throughout August, the succession of ripening fruits and vegetables carried on. The currants, black and red, yielded jam and jelly. The red currant jelly was served with meat or used as a glaze for cakes and tarts. Forced through an icing tip, it made the decorative writing on cakes. A spoonful stirred into stewed fruit gave it a tart piquancy; and it was one of the preserve cupboards most useful relishes. The black currant made a rich, full-flavoured jam or jelly that had no equal spread on buttered toast at the breakfast table.

After the currants were done, the biggest berry crop of all came in — the blueberry, the queen of all Nova Scotia's wild fruits, the easiest to pick, the most plentiful, and the most versatile. Burned over by a beneficent CNR, the railway cuttings of the province provided hundreds of miles of easy pickings; and the children of the province harvested enormous quantities. We brought them home in buckets, and our mothers served them with brown sugar and milk; cooked them in pies; stewed them in grunts; baked them in muffins; and boiled them into jam. Their spicy, woodsy flavour is as unique as their dusty-blue colour and, of all the variations on the blueberry theme, I loved blueberry grunt the best. In many homes, this might be served as a main course and, though mother always considered it a dessert, it is certainly filling enough to need a very slight accompaniment. On our forays after blueberries we would take note of the chokecherry crop; the trees grew wild everywhere, and were laden with mouth-puckering berries. This rather acrid fruit made an excellent jelly if the cherries were picked a little before full ripeness; that is, if the fruit was still red instead of a completely ripe black. As they were small, it took a lot to make enough juice for jelly; but there was no shortage of them and they were easy to pick, simply stripping the bunches off the low bushes. Less fun were the blackberries — in fact picking them was murder, for the bushes were armed with vicious thorns.

But my mother was undaunted, and sallied forth after the blackberries in a leather jacket and old leather gloves with the fingers cut off. We all felt that her efforts were worth it when we ate the blackberry jelly in the comfort of the breakfast-time kitchen; but few could be persuaded to help her in the picking.

She also made a wonderful deep-dish pie, filled with blackberries and apples and served with thick, thick cream. This Devonshire cream was a very special treat which my grandmother sometimes made when the cream-giving cow had outdone herself in production. It took a long time to make and had to be carefully watched; but nothing could equal the sweet, creamy richness of it contrasted with the crispness of pastry and, underlying all, the tang of the apples flavoured with the pungent blackberries. This was August's answer to July's perfect cherry pie. The blackberries were also good and, it must be admitted, less calorie-laden when served with curds. My mother's friend Clara used to make curds, and wonderfully fresh they tasted as compared to commercial cottage cheese. They were good eaten by themselves, too, with a little sprinkle of cinnamon and sugar; they were a dieter's delight although, skinny and calorie unconscious, I couldn't have cared less about that part of it.

Sometimes in our pursuit of wild berries we went "up the Branch" to a spot near a beaver dam. We would leave the adults at their picking and creep off to the edge of the river to watch the beavers. They worked frantically to shore up weak spots in the dam, to cut off little flows, or to deepen the water in their pool, diminished by the August heat. In the pool, we could see the occasional flash of trout; and the beaver, well used to fishermen near their lodges, would carry on working quite close to us. Many of the wild animals were quite tame at this time of year, since the hunting season was still two months off. Deer came down to the river to drink or to lick salt from the rocks at low tide. Porcupines lumbered about, quite oblivious to humans and, occasionally, one would see some raccoons though they were generally shyer.

We had another good opportunity to see wildlife while paddling up the river in a canoe, just at dusk. Our favourite sight was the big bald eagle who lived on the river bank, just above the village. As the canoe entered his "territory" he would take off from his favourite perch, a tall, dead pine tree, and soar overhead, watching us keenly until we had passed through his particular stretch of water. Then, he would go back to his tree and continue watching the water for fish. Around us, on the water, would be the mother ducks with flotillas of tiny ducklings; but, no matter how carefully we tried to drift up on them unawares, the alarm would always be given and all would dive, surfacing after a short interval at an incredible distance. Less nervous were the cranes who stood meditatively in the shallow water, now and then stabbing up a fish, while the sandpipers tore around frantically, like shoppers looking for bargains at a sale.

After sunset, when we had paddled far enough upriver to leave the salt water behind, we would land the canoe and have a supper while waiting for the moon to come up and the tide to turn so we could drift home by moonlight. Strangely enough, I seem to remember more August evenings with high tide at about 9 p.m. and a full moon, than perusal of an almanac and tide table would indicate as reasonable or even possible; but in any case there were lots of them. The favourite supper for these outings was a cornboil. The number of cobs of corn we girls and boys could put away on these occasions was quite incredible; but then so was the goodness of the corn. Golden Bantam, small, rather irregular cobs filled with huge, milky kernels was the best variety. Of all vegetables, corn loses its flavour the quickest after picking, so no supermarket corn can come close to the freshly picked, home-grown product. This is why many people still grow a little corn even if their garden space is strictly limited, just so they can have a "feed" of corn at the peak of its flavour. Mother had a good trick for buttering corn. She would wrap up little pats of butter in squares of gauze from dad's surgery. This little butter ball was rubbed over the corn and more butter stayed on the cob and less dripped off onto the plate; on outdoor cornboils it was even handier.

Another waterborn cookout was the clambake. Then, we headed down-river, toward the bay, on the falling tide. On the sandbars we would spot little breathing holes for the clams and dig for them with spades and forks. It was no use digging with bare hands, for the clams could always dig faster than we could. Muddy to the knees and elbows, we would get a bucket of clams and then wash them. You could never wash well enough, but we always tried! Then, after our fire was built, the clams would be put on an old oven rack over the heat to make them open. They were delicious, if a bit gritty, cooked; but we dared each other to swallow them raw. A particularly large clam was the big, white quahog; and once someone dared my mother to swallow one. Quite unperturbed, she picked up the shell, tipped it into her mouth and gulped. The quahog was gone; and since we had been out-done in our sideshow act by an adult, swallowing live clams lost its savour for the rest of us. The clambakes were lots of fun; but the clams were much better when carried home and fried or made into chowder, for then the sand could be properly washed out of them. We did this by first scrubbing the shells with a stiff brush in lots of running water. Then, the clams were put in a pot without any more water, covered, and cooked till they opened. The clams were taken out of the shells and the black end cut off. They were carefully rinsed in the clam juice, which was then allowed to stand un-disturbed to let the sand settle to the bottom; then, the clear juice was decanted. Sometimes, we filtered it through filter paper for, with cloth, the grit went through. The clams were put back in the juice and they were ready to use.

Less mundane than the rather lowly clam was the scallop. When I was growing up, the scallop beds had not then been established off our shores; when we had scallops they came all the way from Digby and were a great treat. The simplest way of cooking them was dredged in flour and fried, but this required a great deal of care as overheating toughened them. I much preferred it when my mother baked them in the oven. Of course they also made delicous chowder.

The tomatoes would be ripening in large quantities in late August, and they appeared at every meal. Strangely enough, people did not cook with them very much — perhaps because they were so good raw — but my mother did use them in a simple quick soup which was very refreshing, and not heavy on a warm summer evening.

We also needed light desserts at this time of year and, while fresh fruit filled the bill most of the time, my grandmother had a repertoire of cooling and substantial dessert dishes which we all loved. The best was floating island, or, even lighter, lemon snow. Her jellies were good too, quite different from the rubber water which is all most people know as a gelatin dessert. Mama Murray always used fresh fruit juice to make her jellies and she did not make them too stiff; they got their substance from generous amounts of cut-up fruit folded in. She had several elaborate china jelly molds and, turned out of these onto a cut glass dish, the dessert looked as good as it tasted. Naturally, there was the jug of cream from "Moscow" for pouring over it. No, this was not an exotic imported cream, but simply our way of honouring our gallant Russian allies by naming grandmother's cow for their beleaguered capital.

The greater part of my childhood was passed during the war years and, although we suffered no hardships (except for the inevitable telegrams which came to households all across Canada), it was ever present in our consciousness. It did circumscribe our lives in small ways, cutting down travel and throwing us more upon our own resources. Rationing, while imposing no real shortages did cause people to be aware of the amounts of ingredients used; and cutting down on sugar and butter probably meant that, in general, the standard of cooking improved.

Exotics such as bananas and pineapple disappeared. I remember my excitement when we were given a large can of pineapple by a friend from Lunenburg, who got it from a Tancook Island fisherman, who liberated it from an American supply ship that had run aground off the south shore. The mention of Tancook brings to mind the sauerkraut which was the chief product of that rock-ribbed little island. It came in small barrels and had a wonderfully pungent flavour. The Scots of Pictou County had little use for it; but it was a staple for those of German extraction whose cuisine was very different from ours, although we lived only about a hundred miles apart. We liked sauerkraut though and always got some to eat with the oysters which would be available as soon as August gave way to September.

RECIPES — AUGUST

September

SEPTEMBER CAME, and we went back to school! This really wasn't too bad as we usually had the excitement of a new teacher to look forward to. Many of these young teachers came from villages no bigger than our own; but the fact that they did come from "away" broadened our perspectives, and lessened the insularity of our rather confined lives. One teacher in particular, a young Acadian girl from Digby, came to our school where most of the pupils had never known a French, Roman Catholic. In the time that she stayed, simply by being an ordinary, pleasant person, in no way different from ourselves, she broke down the barriers of prejudice and intolerance which ignorance had produced. How and what she taught in the curriculum is forgotten; but the lesson of understanding still remains with many of her pupils.

The return to school was also eased by the fact that we knew a holiday was scheduled for the following week. This was because all schools in the county were closed to allow the children to attend the Pictou Exhibition, the county fair. This was a day-long outing which we enjoyed each in his own way. For my part, I found the barns full of livestock somewhat over-powering, especially in the olfactory sense. Mother was nervous too, con-vinced that I would be kicked by a horse or stepped on by a cow. She needn't have worried; the last thing in the world I wanted was to be any-where near them. Anyhow, we both headed with relief for the main hall where the whole of the lower floor was taken up with the displays of fruit, flowers, and vegetables. The exhibits of handiwork — elaborate em-broideries, hooked mats, and quilts — were displayed along one side of the upstairs; on the other side were the entries in the baking, and preserving contests. Each pie or cake had a piece cut out to show that the judges had indeed sampled each one. There were so many red, blue, and white cards that it sometimes seemed to me that, as in *Alice,* "Everybody has won, and ALL must have prizes."

The day at the Exhibition wound up with the wild thrills of Bill Lynche's travelling sideshow with its breathtaking rides. Back at school the next day, we bragged about the number of times we had ridden on the ferris wheel and wrote compositions entitled "What I Saw At The Fair" or "How to Tell a Good Percheron." After this, the school year really began and we settled down to the serious business of avoiding work and the teacher's eye.

Coming home from school at this time of year meant entering a house redolent with the spicy smell of pickles. Fruit continued to ripen too, and plums, pears, and a few peaches were gathered, bottled, or canned; but the main product seemed to be pickles. Sweet or hot, single or mixed, chows or chutneys — mother made them all. The ripe tomatoes made chili sauce, the green ones, chow. Cucumbers were pickled in brine and in vinegar; onions and beets were spiced and "put down." For some reason I never discovered, jams and jellies were "put up" while pickles were "put down." At our house, everything wound up in the cellar, but the distinction was always maintained. The best pickles of all were mustard pickles, and I would dig through a whole bottle to find the crunchy cauliflower florets that were my especial delight.

I have mentioned oysters; and one day my father would be sure to come home with a potato sack full of them. He loved them, and would sit on the back step with the oyster knife, salt and pepper and the bag at his feet. He wasn't as good at opening them as mother was, and she took her oysters to the kitchen and made oyster stew. Despite her ability to swallow quahogs, she really did not care for uncooked shellfish and preferred her oysters fried or, if left in their shell, gently baked in the oven. This last was my favourite preparation, for I could still have the fun of eating them on the half shell.

All the fresh fruit pies of the summer months didn't dull our appetites for that first long-awaited pie made from the new apple crop. There were a few early August apples but the bulk of the crop came in September — apples from our own trees, from local farmers, and barrels and barrels rolling up from the Annapolis Valley. Duchess and Fameuse, Northern Spy and Gravenstein, Winesap and Russet, each had its own particular flavour and texture, each its own special recipes. There was apple slump, apple dumplings, baked apples, apple fritters, apple crumble, apple cake, and, the cornerstone of every cook's reputation, apple pie. I really think that apple pie has been brought to the peak of perfection in North America. The French make a good one it is true, even though it lacks a top. Their pastry is superb but they can't leave the apples alone. The British, on the other hand, make a pie with no bottom and, while they have the sense to let the apples keep a true flavour, they often make a heavy, doughy pastry which spoils the dish.

On our side of the Atlantic the two-crust pie is better looking and easier to serve; it has enough pastry to balance the filling which is, of course, made from some of the world's best apples — or used to be until government departments urged farmers to cut down trees in the interest of uniformity and shipping quality. However, that may be, "mom's apple pie" deserves better than the supercilious disdain that phrase invokes. The incredible awfulness of cardboard pastry and ersatz filling has made many people forget what true homemade apple pie is like. One taste of the real thing and the sneers would die away. The scoffers would be too busy eating! Every "mom" in our village made apple pie and it must be confessed that some were better than others. I always felt that my mother's deserved to be called the best; and, while I could hardly be called a disinterested judge, I had the feeling that most people who ate it agreed with me. Comparisons are odious and it might be better to say that her pies were perfect.

There were still a couple of jams and jellys left to be put up against the long winter. The windfall apples had of course been made into jelly, reddened and fortified with juice from the berries of the mountain ash or rowan tree. These berries could make jelly all on their own without the addition of apple juice but, though it had beautiful colour and clarity, it was very sour and we preferred to mix it with the apple to make a jelly that was very tart and suitable for serving with game.

The vegetable marrow was the basis for another favourite jam of mine, the rather bland vegetable being flavoured with ginger and lemon. The result was somewhat like a marmalade but with a firmer consistency. Sometimes vegetable marrow was mixed with damson plums to make another very good jam. Peach jam was a favourite of mine, but mother usually preferred to bottle the peaches in syrup. Now that freezing is so easy, the bottled peaches are not so common but they are very good and much more attractive than frozen ones.

While there were no more berries for mother to pick, there were still wild mushrooms available; and she would go out early in the morning to find these at the peak of their flavour. Since they were frequently to be found in pastures, she had to keep a weather eye out for bulls; but that did not deter her and she brought home baskets. We ate some of them sautéed with panbroiled steak, and mother canned the rest. The only two varieties we gathered were the common field mushroom and the puffball. The puffballs were round, golf-ball sized fungi, although occasionally they would grow much larger. I remember one individual, locally famous for his "stretchers," describing the tremendous proportions of a puffball he picked in his orchard. With characteristic hyperbole, he declared that it was so big that it took two pounds of butter to fry it up! No one ever worried about the inclusion of poisonous species, as both field mushrooms and puffballs are quite distinctive. Their flavour is delicate and elusive but considerably stronger than the cultivated button mushroom.

Toward the end of September, pork would begin to replace lamb as the most plentiful meat. Its full, rich flavour was complemented by the stronger-tasting vegetables available at this season; and a roast pork Sunday dinner had a mellow richness well suited to the autumn. As always, mother boned her pork roasts and stuffed them with her savory dressing, a little more heavily spiced now. A squash would be baked in the oven along with the meat, and potatoes would be roasted in the pan itself. When the meat was served, creamy Gravenstein applesauce would accompany it, and strips of crisp crackling would add texture to the plate.

In addition to roast pork, the pig gave us chops which mother baked so that they were always tender and succulent, never hard or dry. Fresh bacon was another treat. This was simply the streaky side meat, thinly sliced, as bacon is, but uncured. It fried like bacon but did not taste at all the same, and was served with potatoes and vegetables rather than with eggs.

By the end of September, the leaves would be at their red and golden best and a drive to Green Hill Lookout would let us see the coloured spectacle over an area of three counties. On the way home, my father would always stop at the spring that flows out of the rock at the base of the hill and is the clearest, coldest, purest water I ever tasted. When King David longed for the water of the well of Bethlehem I am sure it was water such as that of Green Hill.

RECIPES — SEPTEMBER

October

OCTOBER was always a welcome month. The weather was still pleasant, often better than that of September when we were occasionally visited by the tail ends of southern hurricanes, plus some easterlies that the northern ocean brewed up for itself. Besides, October began with a holiday, Thanksgiving, and ended with the second best day of the whole year, Hallowe'en.

At school, the younger children collected maple leaves and pressed them to send away to be judged. I have no idea where these tons of foliage ended up; but we devoutly believed that all went to Ottawa where MacKenzie King, or failing him, Princess Alice, looked at them and picked the best one. What happened to the donor after that we were never told; but we assumed something in the line of a gold printed "certificate" would be issued.

The older scholars would be settling into harness — to the extent that some of them ever settled into anything — and a new teacher would feel sufficiently familiar to be somewhat tolerant of the rising high spirits and rash of practical jokes as Hallowe'en drew closer. The influx of field mice into the warmth of cellars and sheds assured a plentiful supply for enclosing in the teacher's desk or briefcase; while the first fires lit in the potbellied stoves in each room always ensured a rash of smoke and/or stink bombs.

Thanksgiving started off with the Harvest Home service at the little grey Anglican church. This was smaller than the United or Presbyterian houses of worship but it was much prettier. The building itself was graceful and had good proportions; and with its soft, grey-blue walls, bright altar cloths, glowing windows, and shining brass it was, to me, a place of mysterious beauty, accustomed as I was to the austere browns and beiges of our own church, with its interior completely sheathed in varnished hardwood and filled with brown-painted pine pews. No decorations relieved the walls of our church, and the high, wide windows let in a clear, hard light.

Small wonder I liked to attend the Harvest Home service when the Anglican church was filled; and we sang "Come Ye Thankful People Come" and "Bringing in The Sheaves"; and looked at the piles of pumpkins and squash, and the ears of corn and barley.

Next day, at dinner, we would sometimes have turkey; it was not always possible, for not too many farmers raised them. If we couldn't get turkey, then a big capon was cooked instead. Because it was Thanksgiving, mother cooked as many vegetables as possible so our plates were mounded high. I liked turkey because it meant two kinds of dressing, one in the body and another in the breast cavity. The gravy mother made with her turkey was especially delicious because she usually cooked a roast of pork together with the turkey in the same pan. The fat from the pork basted the turkey and kept it from drying out; and at the same time the glazing on the pan was browner and richer, giving much better gravy. The cold pork on the days following added variety to the inevitable turkey leftovers. Since we were a small family, there was always lots of leftover meat when we had a turkey and mother made the most of it. The best would, of course, be sliced and served cold but the scraps were the basis of a number of dishes, all of them excellent. There were turkey croquettes (a real "company" dish), turkey turnovers, turkey pie, and finally turkey soup, made from the carcass. These were in the future on Thanksgiving itself, and I was too busy loading my plate with roast turkey to look ahead to its later incarnations. With the roast turkey, was the wonderful cranberry sauce made by my grandmother's method. She produced the most perfect cranberry sauce, every berry round and unbroken; and it was so easy. Her method is described in the recipe for Perfect Cranberry Sauce. Buttered parsnips, mashed potatoes, squash, brussel sprouts, all would be served; but mother wouldn't open any of her bottled and canned vegetables just yet. There was a long winter ahead! For dessert, mother would make, not a pumpkin, but a squash pie; the latter is less coarse and heavy and makes a pie filling with a better texture. Mother used her spices judiciously and never let one dominate over the others, so the flavour of her pie was subtle and quite unusual. A big bowl of whipped cream accompanied the pie to be slathered over each helping. Mother would use pumpkin to make a spicy, steamed pudding which was an October favourite; and some of the other women used leftover pumpkin and squash to make muffins. The pumpkins were so big that often even a large family would have trouble using one all up. An old lady who had fallen downstairs and hurt herself told me that, as she was flying down the stairs, she had time to think that the way they used to break the pumpkins was to throw them down the cellar stairs; and she wondered if her head would split like some of them. Fortunately, it did not and she was able to impress us all with her ability to speculate on her probable fate, while shooting through the air.

With Thanksgiving behind us, preparations for Hallowe'en became more exciting. As far as costumes went, we had to make our own. The two most important points were that, one, they should be warm; and two, that they should cover us from top to toe, for everyone in the village knew us well and could guess our identities if they glimpsed so much as an ear. Some of us bought false faces at the store, while others used burnt cork or stocking masks. We wore big work gloves and outsized rubber boots, and a few made elaborate wigs out of frayed rope. Meanwhile, our mothers were busy making the cookies and candy for giving away, for very few of the treats were "store bought." Finally, the great night arrived. Supper was cleared away early for the smallest children started coming as soon as it was dark. The treats would be put on the kitchen table and soon the first knocks would sound. Each party would be invited in and the children would sit around the kitchen, heads down, eyes lowered, responding with nods, grunts, and occasional giggles as the adults tried to guess their identities. While this exercise was taking place, the treats were passed around and each child took something and ate it on the spot. It was not until I was almost grown up that the practice of carrying bags around became prevalent; and I remember the shocked comments the first time a child showed up carrying one. Since each child only took what he could eat, the amount each household was required to serve was not that great, and the quality was much higher. We knew from year to year what to expect at different houses. A great bowl of doughnuts was my grandmother's Hallowe'en treat, while my mother made chocolate fudge. Molasses toffee, butterscotch humbugs, brown-sugar fudge, homemade turkish delight, toffee apples, and huge cookies were offered to us at other houses. If the householders did not guess your name, it was considered rather bad form to leave without revealing yourself.

Later in the evening, as the younger children would make for home, the older ones would take their place, together with a few adults who, for an hour or so, would put aside their staid, everyday personalities and enjoy themselves. Long after the last lamp had been put out and all the treats had been eaten, the tricks would be played by the older boys. Every moveable set of front or back steps would be pulled away; a few outhouses would be pushed over; the rope for the school bell would be cut; and a scarecrow would be hanged from a board on the bridge. Gates were removed, and garden ornaments hidden; and, of course, somebody's cow would turn up to be milked next morning, painted bright blue. It was all pretty harmless and nobody seemed to mind very much. In a small place, where everyone was well known, it was a tremendous thrill to be anonymous for that short time, and everyone seemed to enjoy and encourage the children's fun. Later, when the children no longer came in but only stood at the door and demanded handouts, much of the pleasure disappeared.

In addition to the plenitude of the Thanksgiving feast and the sweet satiety of Hallowe'en, October had one other contribution to the seasonal variety of our table; namely, game. As my father had carried his fishing rod with him on his calls during the spring, now he kept his gun handy in case he would spot a flock of partridge. He seldom had time to go out deer hunting but many of his patients did, and we were often given gifts of venison, usually steaks but occasionally roasts as well. Unlike the English, who hang game until it is very "high," we preferred game hung a minimum amount of time. Partridge should be hung for three or four days only and then roasted. They are apt to be dry and are best cooked in a casserole. Venison from a fairly young animal should hang about two weeks. If the animal has been properly butchered after it is shot, venison is, of all meats, incomparably the best, whether panbroiled, roasted, or stewed. Unless the animal is old, it is not necessary to marinate it; however, if a marinade is required, not only should the meat be marinated for twenty-four hours, but the cooking time should also be increased.

The other type of game which we enjoyed was wild duck. Some of the duck which lived in the area were somewhat fishy tasting, and it was birds from the flocks migrating from inland that provided the best eating. Wild duck should not be hung for more than two days. Compared to their domestic cousins, they are quite lean and their rich, dark meat has a magnificent flavour.

RECIPES — OCTOBER

November

NOVEMBER WAS A DULL, DARK MONTH, and everyone was much occupied with preparations for the winter. Any house that did not possess a heating system was banked to keep out the cold drafts. A popular dish of salt cod and potatoes was called "house banking," possibly referring to the fact that many people ordered dried salt cod in sufficient quantities to serve that purpose. Salt cod was certainly common winter fare; but, when properly treated, it was amazingly good too, and every housewife had a repertoire of dishes based upon it — everything from codfish balls to a delectable concoction in which the fish was mixed with eggs and cream and poured over thick slices of toasted, homemade bread. Nothing plebeian about that dish!

Both my mother and father had their birthdays in November, but adults never celebrated birthdays much; a present or two, some cards from old friends — that was all. Perhaps, if dad was not busy, we might drive into town to a movie or to do the Christmas shopping. Since many gifts were made at home, usually beautifully-knit sweaters and socks, the materials had to be purchased early. Also, the ingredients for the orgy of Christmas baking had to be collected. November saw the compounding of the two great Christmas cakes, one dark and one light, and an enormous stone crock of mincemeat. Peel was candied for the cakes, and pounds of raisins and currants had to be picked over.

Mother always bought the raisins herself for, somehow, my father could never grasp the distinction between seeded and seedless raisins; so it was no use asking him to pick up a few pounds when he was in town. The seedless raisins were easier to use but it was the big, sticky, seeded ones that imparted the full madeira-like flavour to mother's cakes. They required the most patient picking over to ensure that no stray seeds lurked to break the teeth; and mother invented the pleasant fiction that my "little" fingers and "sharp" eyes could do the job better than hers. I never believed that; but I was afraid that if I didn't do it she might decide not to make mincemeat — and that was a disaster I was unwilling to risk. So I picked and snipped at the sticky things, helped on by a spoonful of candied citron whenever mother's back was turned. Mother could safely trust me among the raisins, dates, cherries, and figs; but I was a confirmed citron thief by age five and got worse and worse as the years went by. Even today, I will steal citron from my own pantry shelves and then have to buy a fresh supply for my cakes.

Gingerbread cookies, which needed to ripen, and brandy snaps, which kept well, were also made in November; but one thing that was not part of mother's traditional Christmas cooking was plum pudding. I don't know why this was but we never had it. One of my aunts did though. She had married an Englishman and had her mother-in-law's recipe; and of all Christmas puddings, Mrs. Smith's, as made by my Aunt "Babe" was the peak of Dickensian perfection.

While all this baking was going on, the everyday meals still had to be prepared. Since the kitchen stove now burned all day there was, at all times, a slow oven available to give the bean crock the long day's cooking required. It was a time too for pot roasts and braised meats, and heavy steamed puddings, and suet dumplings. After supper, we would settle down to long evenings of monopoly and croquinole, while our mothers and aunts knitted and crocheted furiously against the approaching Christmas season.

If my grandmother was making one of her biannual visits to Montreal, a huge parcel would arrive containing things which mother had asked her to get for me. There would be a new snowsuit, or else what mother regarded as the height of juvenile chic, a Red River coat. Red River coats were not at all common in rural Nova Scotia and, since I felt that mine made me conspicuous, I hated it as much as mother loved it. One year, in addition to the coat, Mama Murray included a pair of red, knitted leggings and a red touque from which depended a long string with a pom-pom on the end of it. The sight of this provoked rebellion. I could never hold up my head if that monstrosity were placed upon it! Talk of red rags before bulls! If I walked up to school, past all the boys, with that thing on, I could never survive the teasing. "Nonsense!" said my mother. "It looks perfectly lovely with that coat. So smart." Smart it may have been, but my schoolmates thought it was the funniest thing they ever saw. Fortunately for my peace of mind, there was a strong wind that day; and on my way home, while I was crossing the bridge, it blew off my head and was lost forever.

The last day of November was my friend's birthday, and this always seemed to coincide with the first snowstorm of the season. After school, we would go up to her house for her birthday party, and when the last game had been played, and the birthday cake eaten, we would leave the big, warm kitchen for a white, snow-clogged walk home. It was winter at last and Christmas was coming!

RECIPES — NOVEMBER

December

EARLY IN DECEMBER, the Christmas preparations would move into high gear. The teachers would get together and plan the Christmas concert, which involved tremendous preparation of costumes, learning of "pieces," and practising of drills and choruses. Every one of the young children had to have a part, no matter how small; and after it was all over Santa Claus would come and see that everyone got a present. Some of the Sunday schools would also arrange parties and/or pageants, and there was much stitching of angels' wings and fashioning of shepherds' crooks. Most other costumes were made of crepe paper — wonderful, colourful stuff that could be stitched, ruffled, pleated, fluted, and otherwise tortured into costumes representing everything from snowflakes to stockings. The proprietor of our little stationery store and soda fountain was a master at dealing with this stuff, and fashioned elaborate Christmas window displays in his little store, as well as helping with the costumes for the concert.

On the night of the affair, usually the Friday before Christmas, the whole village would come to the United church hall, a large building which had been the Methodist church before "Union." Every "act" on the program would receive a full meed of applause; and afterwards we would all be assured that we had "done well." It was a wonderful and exciting time for us youngsters and, simple though the setting was, some of the magic of "live theatre" came through to us.

The master of ceremonies was usually one of the ministers, and Santa Claus was always Jim MacDonald; instead of a red suit, he wore a raccoon coat with a beard and wig of carefully frayed rope. The candies we got were Christmas candy, seen at no other time of year. There were long curls of red and green "ribbon" candy, surely the prettiest of all confections, and barley sugar "toys." These were red or yellow shapes ranging in size from small pieces that would fit comfortably in the mouth to huge horses, dogs, and bears, weighing a pound or more, which had to be broken with a hammer into smaller pieces that would provide hours of contented sucking.

Mother would augment these store-bought candies with some homemade ones as well; but the great bulk of her December baking would consist of cookies. With the cakes out of the way in November, the December days could be filled with cookie baking. Nevertheless, there was one last cake to produce — a large, round marble cake. The almond paste and fondant for the icing of the fruit cakes had to be made as well, and in those days, before blenders, the almond paste was a long, tedious job. Again, my fingers were called upon, this time to slip the skins off the almonds, blanched in hot water, or off the filberts, roasted in a hot oven. Mother's brass nutcracker in the shape of a crocodile was great fun to use. You put a walnut or a Brazil nut in his mouth, pushed down on his tail, and his jaws crunched down on the nut and cracked the shell. Mother had a smart trick for loosening the shells of Brazil nuts so that the meats came out whole. It is described in the recipe for Brazil Nut Cookies. The walnuts were used to make all sorts of cookies; two of the best were Portugal squares and a dainty, buttery little lemon cookie we always called Aunt Jean's Christmas cherries. Of course there were pounds and pounds of shortbread. My grandmother and Maisie MacIntosh were the best shortbread makers in the village, I thought. Mama Murray made hers with white sugar, Maisie used brown; but both were equally good. Mama Murray laid the fine side of the nutmeg grater on top of hers to give a distinctive little pimpled pattern over the surface. For some reason, these were never called shortbread but always Scotch cookies; but a shortbread by whatever name is still the best and richest of all cookies.

As the magic day drew nearer, dad would make a trip up to the West Branch where he had spotted a nice stand of Christmas trees, while hunting or fishing. He would bring home a beautiful little fir, always perfectly formed and symmetrical, fresh and sweetly pungent — but never, never big enough to suit me. Since our house had cozy low ceilings, I don't know where I thought we could put the forest giant of my dreams; but, by the time the tree was brought in and decorated, I was reconciled to its stature. And each year the tree was more beautiful than the last!

The night before Christmas, our living room always seemed the most beautiful place in the world, with an enormous log of mountain hardwood burning in the big, grey, sandstone fireplace and the tree, glowing with light, standing in the front window. My cat stared longingly through the glass dining room door at the tree, which it was his annual ambition to demolish, and my father sat by the fire listening to the music on the radio. My mother was not in this chaming picture because she was in the kitchen until late, late on Christmas Eve, getting things ready for the great dinner the next day. Dinner on Christmas Day had to be at noon, so much of the preparation had to be done the night before. Mince pies were made; dressing compounded; the ducks (for that was our traditional meal) , and all the vegetables prepared. Long after I had hung up my stocking and gone to bed, mother would carry on in the kitchen to ensure that our Christmas dinner was perfect.

When I hung up my stocking on Christmas Eve, there were no presents under the tree — not one. But very early the next morning, when I came downstairs, there was a whole mountain of presents, plus my long, lumpy stocking. And beside the fireplace, where I had put the first piece cut off the fruitcake, together with a carrot for the reindeer, there was an empty plate and glass. Santa had been; all was well; and I could go back to my warm bed, dragging my stocking filled with treasure!

After everybody got up, we opened all our presents, listened to King George, and then had the dinner. What a dinner — the best of the whole year! Mother's idea of serving duck was a very good one, especially if Christmas dinner is served at midday. Unfortunately, it only works for relatively small numbers, for two ducks will serve eight people at most. However, if the number of people expected at the table falls within this limit, the short cooking time required makes duck an excellent choice. The appearance, on mother's big platter, of the brace of duck, glazed with orange marmalade, and surrounded with orange cups filled with sparkling red cranberry, was beautiful to see. They were easy to serve too for, instead of carving them, dad simply cut them in four and served each person with one quarter of a bird. There is too much fat on duck to stuff it with bread dressing, and the goose at New Year would have potato dressing; so mother cooked the bread dressing in a bowl, and filled the ducks with quartered oranges and a few juniper berries which flavoured the flesh most beautifully.

With the platter, was a regiment of vegetable dishes containing every kind of vegetable our root cellar and preserve cupboard could deliver, plus a large gravy boat filled with orange gravy. This was not the orange sauce of the classic French cuisine, but a richer, fuller-bodied concoction, well able to support the flavour of the giblets swimming in it. Since we began the meal with tomato soup, everyone was pretty full before dessert even came along; but belts were eased, and room was found for mince pie; and perhaps even for a slice of fruitcake.

As soon as dinner was over, all the children of the village headed out of doors to try the new skates and flexible flyers we had got for Christmas. We skated, coasted, and visited until dark; then, we came home, wonder of wonders — hungry.

One other nice thing about duck for Christmas is that there is not the eternal succession of leftovers; instead, the carcasses find their way, the very next day, into the soup pot to make duck soup. This is a hot and nourishing dish, just the thing for cold children coming in after an afternoon of playing in the snow. Our snowsuits were made of heavy blanket cloth and the snow clung to them in great, heavy lumps. After a few minutes outdoors, a child could accumulate several pounds of snow and ice on his person, and it was necessary to be swept down with a broom before entering the house. These preliminaries over with, it was marvellous to come into the warm kitchen and "sit in" to a big bowl of duck soup. It was so good that I always forgot to pick out the pieces of turnip — an invariable practice of mine with all mother's other soups.

Very soon the year was over. The brand new Bank of Nova Scotia calendar with the picture of a sailing ship was ready to go up; the goose for New Year's dinner was hanging on the back porch, frozen; the old year was passing. And, on the last night of the old year, the ladies set out their best dishes, laden with cakes and cookies; dressed up in their best clothes; and sat in the parlour with their daughters, while the men and boys went out to mark the old Scots custom of first footing. Actually, most of the calls were paid before midnight; but, after the passing bell rang, the first visitor of the New Year had to be a dark-haired man to bring good fortune to the house in the coming year. After all the houses had been blessed in this fashion, the village went to sleep, looking forward to another year of placid enjoyment of the country's good things.

RECIPES — DECEMBER

PART 2
Recipes

Beverages and Confectionery

COCOA

¼ cup (50 mL) cocoa
¼ cup (50 mL) sugar
tiny pinch of salt
2 cups (400 mL) water

1½ cups (300 mL) evaporated milk
½ tsp (2 mL) vanilla extract
whipped cream

Mix cocoa, sugar and salt. Add water. Bring to a boil; boil for 3 minutes. Add milk and reheat gently, whisking continually. Heat to steaming point. Add vanilla. Serve, garnished with whipped cream.

LEMONADE SYRUP

6 large lemons
5 lb (2 kg) sugar
2 oz (50 g) citric acid
1 oz (25 g) tartaric acid
½ oz (12 g) Epsom salts
3½ pt (2 L) boiling water

Grate the peel from all the lemons and reserve. Squeeze the lemons. Combine sugar, lemon peel, lemon juice, citric acid, tartaric acid, Epsom salts. Pour boiling water over; stir until sugar and salts are dissolved. Let stand till cool; strain and bottle. Keep in refrigerator. For delicious lemonade, add cold water and ice, with a twist of fresh lemon peel, to sufficient syrup to taste.

LIME JUICE

1 cup (250 mL) unsweetened lime juice
5 cups (1250 mL) ice water
1 cup (250 mL) sugar, or, to taste

Mix lime juice and ice water; add sugar until desired sweetness is reached.
Do not make too sweet. Keep refrigerated for summer refresher.

RASPBERRY VINEGAR

sugar
1 lb (500 g) ripe raspberries
1 qt (1 L) white wine vinegar

Clean and hull raspberries. Pour the vinegar over them and let them stand
for 2 weeks. Strain through a jelly bag. Weigh the liquid and add double
this weight of sugar. Do not stir but let the sugar dissolve gradually. When
the sugar has all dissolved, bottle the vinegar. Pour ⅓ cup (85 mL) vinegar
over ice in a glass and add ice water to desired strength.

ROOT BEER

1 bottle Hires root beer extract
4 lb (1.8 kg) sugar
3 gal (13.5 L) lukewarm water
½ tsp (2 mL rounded) dried yeast

Add the yeast to 1 cup (250 mL) of the water with 1 tsp (5 mL) of sugar.
Set aside. In a large container mix the remaining sugar and the extract.
Rinse the bottle of extract with some of the water, as otherwise some
extract will remain in the bottle. Add the rest of the water and stir until
all the sugar is dissolved. Add the cup of yeast mixture. Fill clean bottles to
within ½ in. (1 cm) of the top with the mixture and cap them. *Use bottles
previously used for carbonated soft drinks. Do not use wine bottles or juice
bottles* which will not withstand pressure. Lay bottles on their sides in a
warm place above 75°F (23°C), and leave 3-4 days. Store bottles in a cool
place and refrigerate before drinking. Note: The cost of this summer
beverage is about 3 or 4 cents per 10 oz (284 mL) glass. Use crown caps with
a capper, available at hardware and winemakers' supply stores. Readers
should be aware that this recipe produces a beverage with a slight alcoholic
content.

BARLEY SUGAR

1 cup (250 mL) pearl barley
5 qt (5 L) water
2 lb (1 kg) sugar
2 tbsp (30 mL) white corn syrup
1¼ cups (300 mL) water

Place barley in the 5 qt (5 L) of water and cook gently for 5 hours. Strain off liquid, which will be a white, jelly-like substance. Set aside. In a heavy pan, melt sugar and corn syrup in water and bring to boil. Skim carefully, and do not allow scum to stick to side of pan. Cook to 230°F (110°C). Measure 1 cup (250 mL) of reserved barley water liquid and add to the sugar syrup. Do this carefully to avoid spitting. Stir once gently and cook again to 310°F (155°C). Pour into oiled barley sugar molds, or pour on oiled marble, and cut in strips. This is tricky candy to make as it is very apt to crystallize.

BUTTERSCOTCH

¾ lb (300 g) brown sugar
¼ lb (100 g) glucose
6 tbsp (70 mL) butter
½ cup plus 2 tbsp (130 mL) water

Dissolve sugar in water and add glucose. Stir in the butter and bring to a boil. Boil, undisturbed, to 280°F (137°C). Brush down sides of pan with fork wrapped in strip of damp cheesecloth. Pour into a greased pan. Let set and mark into squares with oiled knife.

BROWN SUGAR FUDGE

2½ cups (625 mL) firmly packed brown sugar
pinch of salt
1 tbsp (15 mL) corn syrup
1 tbsp (15 mL) butter
¾ cup (190 mL) milk
2 tsp (10 mL) vanilla extract

Combine sugar, salt, syrup, butter, and milk in heavy pan. Cook slowly, stirring till sugar dissolves. Bring to boil and cook without stirring to 238°F (112°C). Remove from heat, cool to lukewarm. Add vanilla and beat until thickened. Pour into a greased pan. Cut in squares when cool.

CHERRY ALMOND FUDGE

5 cups (1200 mL) white sugar
⅔ cup (160 mL) heavy cream
1 cup (240 mL) milk
4 tbsp (60 mL) white corn syrup

¼ tsp (1 mL) salt
1 tsp (5 mL) almond extract
½ cup (120 mL) halved glacé cherries

Combine sugar, cream, milk, syrup, and salt in heavy saucepan. Cook, stirring, until boiling. Continue cooking to soft ball, 234°F (112°C). Remove from heat; cool to 110°F (43°C). Add almond — vanilla may be substituted if almond flavour is not liked — and beat until candy is dull. Fold in cherries; pour into greased tin. Cut in squares and decorate with additional cherries.

BEST CHOCOLATE FUDGE

4 oz (100 g) bitter chocolate
6 oz can (150 g) evaporated milk
6 oz (150 g) marshmallows
1 cup (200 mL) brown sugar
½ cup (100 mL) white sugar

¼ tsp (1 mL) salt
¼ cup (50 mL) butter
12 oz (300 g) semisweet chocolate
1 tsp (5 mL) vanilla extract

Chop bitter and semisweet chocolate into small pieces; set aside. Combine milk, marshmallows, brown and white sugar, and salt. Bring to boil and cook hard for 5 minutes. Add chocolate and stir till melted. Add vanilla. Beat till cool and turn into buttered pan.

DIVINITY FUDGE

3 cups (575 mL) white sugar
½ cup (110 mL) light corn syrup
½ cup (110 mL) water
2 egg whites
1 tsp (4 mL) vanilla extract
pinch of salt

Boil sugar, syrup, and water to 244°F (117°C). Whip egg whites with salt until stiff. Pour in syrup in a thin stream, beating egg whites all the while. Add vanilla. Drop by spoonfuls on waxed paper.

HUMBUGS

1 lb (500 g) brown sugar
3 tbsp (45 mL) butter
2 tsp (10 mL) corn syrup
2 tsp (10 mL) molasses

¼ tsp (1 mL heaping) cream of tartar
½ cup plus 2 tbsp (155 mL) water
2 drops of oil of peppermint

Boil all ingredients except peppermint to a hard crack, 290°F (143°C). Remove from heat and let stand 1 minute. Pour onto a marble slab and add peppermint. Let cool. Oil hands and, when cool enough to handle, pull the toffee till smooth and light. Pull out and cut in ½ in. (1 cm) pieces.

MOLASSES TAFFY

½ cup (125 mL) molasses
1½ cup (375 mL) sugar
½ cup (125 mL) water
¼ tsp (1 mL) cream of tartar

4 tbsp (60 mL) melted butter
pinch of soda
1½ tbsp (23 mL) vinegar

Cook molasses, sugar, water, and vinegar to boiling. Add cream of tartar. Cook to 290°F (143°C). Add butter and soda. Pour on greased marble slab. When cool enough to handle, pull until smooth and light.

TOFFEE

½ cup (120 mL) sugar
⅔ cup (160 mL) brown sugar
6 tbsp (90 mL) corn syrup
⅔ cup (160 mL) cream

pinch of salt
2 tbsp (30 mL) butter
½ tsp (2 mL) vanilla extract

Combine first five ingredients in a heavy pan and cook to 244°F (117°C). Add butter and remove from heat. Add vanilla. Stir but do not beat. Spread on oiled marble slab. Cool and cut in squares.

ANNIE'S TURKISH DELIGHT

2 envelopes plain gelatin
⅓ cup (85 mL) lemon juice
½ cup (125 mL) cornstarch
⅓ cup (85 mL) cold water
2 cups (500 mL) sugar

1 cup (250 mL) water
2 tbsp (30 mL) corn syrup
2 tsp (10 mL) rose water
1 or 2 drops red food coloring
icing sugar

Boil sugar, water, and corn syrup to soft ball. Meanwhile, mix the cornstarch with the cold water and cook till clear and very thick. Soften the gelatin in the lemon juice. Remove syrup from heat; add gelatin mixture, and cornstarch mixture, and stir until melted. Add colouring and rose water. Cover the bottom of an 8 in. (20 cm) pie plate with icing sugar. Pour in syrup, sprinkle with more icing sugar. Let set for 2-3 hours. Cut in squares and serve.

CANDIED PEEL

peels from 6 oranges, 3 grapefruit,
   8 lemons
sugar
water
3 tbsp (45 mL) salt

Remove the peels from the fruit in quarters. Soak the peels overnight in
3 qt (3 L) of water to which salt has been added. Drain. Place different
peels in separate saucepans to keep flavours from blending. Cover with cold
water; bring to boil and drain. Repeat three more times; then simmer until
peels are tender. Drain and weigh the peels; add to each an equal amount of
sugar and ½ cup (125 mL) water. Bring to boil, and simmer until peels
are transparent. Remove and drain on rack. Roll in sugar and leave on tray
to dry. Cut to desired shape and size according to the use to be made of
the candied peel. Store tightly covered.

Breads, Quick Breads, Cereals, and Pasta

WHITE BREAD

2 packages or cakes of yeast
1 cup (250 mL) warm water, 85°F (30°C)
1 tsp (5 mL) sugar
4 cups (1 L) water — milk may be
    substituted for half of the water

4 tsp (20 mL) salt
2 tbsp (30 mL) shortening,
    melted and cooled
10-12 cups (2.5-3 L) flour,
    more or less

Dissolve sugar in the warm water in a large bowl. Stir in the yeast and let stand 10 minutes. This is known as "proofing" the yeast. Continue by stirring in 2 cups (500 mL) of flour. This will give a dry, rough mixture. Cover tightly and leave 4 or 5 hours at room temperature in a draft-free place. Uncover, and the mixture will have formed a loose, spongy batter. Stir in the rest of the water, salt, shortening, and 2 cups (500 mL) more flour. Beat well. Stir in about 6 cups (1.5 L) more flour until a soft dough which cleans the bowl is made. Turn out onto floured board and knead for 10 minutes adding more flour if dough gets sticky. Grease large bowl lightly and place dough in bowl, turning it to coat dough with grease. Cover tightly and leave to rise in a warm place, 85°F (30°C), for about 1½ hours. Turn out dough, divide into four and shape into loaves; place in well-greased loaf pans. Leave to rise until double — about 1 hour — covered with a tea towel. Bake in 400° oven for 25-30 minutes. Remove from pans and cool on racks away from drafts.

ROLLED OATS BREAD

2 packages yeast
½ cup (125 mL) lukewarm water
pinch of sugar
1 cup (250 mL) rolled oats
2 cups (500 mL) boiling water

½ cup (125 mL) molasses
⅓ cup (85 mL) melted shortening
1 tbsp (15 mL) salt
1 egg, beaten
5-6 cups (1250-1500 mL) flour

Place rolled oats in large bowl with molasses, salt, and shortening. Pour on boiling water. Stir. Let stand till lukewarm. Meanwhile, proof yeast in lukewarm water with sugar. When rolled oat mixture is cooled right down, add egg and then proofed yeast. Stir in 2 cups (500 mL) of flour and beat well. Stir in enough extra flour to give a soft dough which can be kneaded. Knead 10 minutes on lightly floured board. Place in greased bowl. Let rise till double. Shape in two loaves; place in greased pans. Let rise till double. Bake 50-60 minutes in 325° oven.

EASTER BREAD

1½ cups (375 mL) water
½ cup (125 mL) melted butter, cooled
2 tsp (10 mL) salt
½ cup (125 mL) sugar
2 packages yeast
¼ cup (60 mL) lukewarm water
½ tsp (2 mL) ground nutmeg

1 tsp (5 mL) allspice
1 tsp (5 mL) caraway seeds
2 cups (500 mL) whole wheat flour
3-4 cups (750-1000 mL) white flour
½ cup (125 mL) currants
1 cup (250 mL) seedless raisins

Proof yeast in lukewarm water with 1 tsp (5 mL) of the sugar. Combine 1½ cups (375 mL) water with butter and remaining sugar; add the proofed yeast, the salt, and the whole wheat flour mixed with the spices. Beat well, and add enough white flour to make a soft dough. Turn out on floured board and knead 10 minutes. Put in a buttered bowl and cover. Let rise till double. Turn out, punch down, and work in raisins and currants. Divide dough in two and shape into loaves. Put into two greased loaf pans and leave to rise till double. Brush loaves with a little melted butter. Bake 50 minutes in 375° oven. Turn out and cool on rack.

BROWN BREAD

1 package or cake of yeast
2½ cups (625 mL) water
1 cup (250 mL) graham flour
1½ cup (375 mL) bran
1 tbsp (15 mL) salt

½ cup (125 mL) molasses
2 tbsp (30 mL) shortening, melted
  and cooled
5-6 cups (1.25-1.5 L) all purpose flour

Proof yeast in lukewarm water with a pinch of sugar. Add graham flour, bran, molasses, salt, and melted shortening. Beat in 2 cups (500 mL) all purpose flour and beat well. Add sufficient extra flour to make a soft dough. Knead 10 minutes. Place in greased bowl and let rise covered for 1½ hours or until double. Punch down and shape into two loaves and place in two 9 x 5 x 3 in. (22 x 12 x 7 cm) loaf pans. Let rise 1 hour or till double. Bake 1 hour in 350° oven. Turn out loaves on rack and brush with melted butter.

ROLLS

1 cup (250 mL) milk	1 tsp (5 mL) salt
¼ cup (60 mL) shortening	1 beaten egg white
1¼ cup (300 mL) lukewarm water	1 package yeast
1½ tbsp (25 mL) sugar	3½-5 cups (825-1250 mL) flour

Scald milk. Proof yeast in water to which the sugar has been added. Add shortening and salt to hot milk and stir to melt. Cool and add to proofed yeast mixture. Add egg white and stir in 1 cup (250 mL) of flour. Beat well. Add extra flour until a soft dough is formed, and knead on lightly floured board until dough is satiny. Place in greased covered bowl and let rise till doubled. Punch down; shape into twenty-four rolls in greased pan. Let rise till doubled. Bake in 375° oven for 30 minutes.

SOFT ROLLS

2 cups (450 mL) flour
1 tsp (5 mL) salt
2 tbsp (30 mL) butter or lard
½ package yeast
½ cup plus 2 tbsp (150 mL) warm milk
2 tbsp (30 mL) lukewarm water

Proof the yeast in water with a pinch of sugar. Combine flour and salt in a bowl and rub in the fat. Add milk and proofed yeast and mix to a soft dough. Cover the bowl and leave to rise till double in bulk. Turn out on a well-floured board and knead 10 minutes. Shape into six long rolls about 4 in. (10 cm) long by 1 in. (2.5 cm) in diameter. Place on greased cookie sheet. Cover and leave to rise in a warm place for 20 minutes. Dust with flour and bake 15 minutes in 425° oven.

BROWN ROLLS

1 package yeast
1 cup (250 mL) water
1 tbsp (15 mL) sugar
2 tbsp (30 mL) shortening
2 tsp (10 mL) salt
1 cup (250 mL) milk
2 cups (500 mL) whole wheat flour
3-4 cups (750-1000 mL) white flour

Proof yeast in warm water and 1 tsp (5 mL) sugar. Scald milk and add shortening, rest of sugar, and salt. Stir to melt shortening; cool. Add to yeast and stir in whole wheat flour. Beat well. Add sufficient white flour to make a soft dough and knead until smooth. Grease a bowl and place dough in it and leave to rise 1½ hours or until double. Punch down and shape into twenty-four rolls in 8 x 12 in. (20 x 30 cm) pan. Let rise until double and bake 25-30 minutes in 375° oven. Remove, brush with melted butter, and cool on rack.

MAPLE BUNS

1 package yeast	½ tsp (2 mL) salt
2 tbsp (30 mL) lukewarm water	½ cup (125 mL) maple cream
1 cup (250 mL) water	½ cup (125 mL) chopped walnuts
½ cup (125 mL) sugar	2 tbsp (30 mL) soft butter
2 tbsp (30 mL) butter	¾ cup (175 mL) maple syrup
1 egg, beaten	¾ cup (175 mL) chopped walnuts
4 cups (1000 mL) all purpose flour	½ cup (125 mL) melted butter
	pinch of salt

Proof yeast in lukewarm water with 1 tsp (5 mL) of the sugar. Put the cup of water, rest of sugar, butter and ½ tsp (2mL) salt in a saucepan and heat till butter is melted. Cool; add proofed yeast and egg. Stir in enough flour to make a soft dough. Refrigerate overnight in a greased, covered bowl. Next day, roll dough into an 18 x 8 in. (45 x 20 cm) rectangle. Combine maple cream, ½ cup (125 mL) walnuts, and 2 tbsp (30 mL) butter in a blender. Spread on the dough and roll up like a jelly roll. You have a roll 18 in. (45 cm) long. Cut into eighteen slices. Combine maple syrup, walnuts, butter, and salt. Divide among eighteen large muffin tins and place a slice of dough on top of mixture, cut side down. Let rise covered for 30 minutes, and bake 20 minutes in 375° oven. Turn out and serve warm.

HOT CROSS BUNS

4 cups (1000 mL) flour	1 package yeast
1 tsp (5 mL) salt	¼ cup (65 mL) tepid water
½ tsp (2 mL) cinnamon	½ cup (125 mL) butter
¼ tsp (1 mL) nutmeg	1 cup (250 mL) scalded milk
¼ tsp (1 mL) allspice	2 eggs
3 tbsp (50 mL) sugar	1 cup (250 mL) currants
1 egg yolk	

Proof yeast in tepid water with 1 tsp (5 mL) of sugar. Add rest of sugar to scalded milk, and add butter. Stir to melt butter and cool mixture to lukewarm. Beat eggs. In large bowl, sift spices and salt into flour. Make a well, and stir in proofed yeast, cooled milk, and eggs. Mix to a dough and knead till smooth and satiny. Let rise till double in a greased, covered bowl. Take a ball of dough about 2 in. (5 cm) in diameter and set aside covered. Turn the rest out on board and knead in the currants, ¼ cup (65 mL) at a time. Shape dough into balls about 1½-2 in. (3-5 cm) in diameter. Place 2 in. (5 cm) apart, on greased baking sheet. With a sharp knife cut a cross on top of each bun. Leave to rise, covered with a tea towel for 20 minutes, or till double. Beat egg yolk and brush the buns with this glaze, carefully avoiding the crosses. Roll the reserved dough into thin strips, half the diameter of a pencil. Lay two strips in each cross. Leave 5 minutes more and then bake in 450° oven for 15 or 20 minutes.

BOSTON BROWN BREAD

1 cup (250 mL) flour
1 cup (250 mL) whole wheat flour
1 cup (250 mL) cornmeal
1 tsp (5 mL) soda

1 tsp (5 mL) baking powder
1 tsp (5 mL) salt
¾ cup (185 mL) molasses

Mix dry ingredients; add molasses and milk. Pour into well-greased tins, filling two-thirds full — 1 lb (500 g) coffee cans are good. Cover with lids, or foil, and place on rack in a steamer. Pour boiling water to come halfway up, and steam 3 hours.

CORN BREAD

1 cup (250 mL) cornmeal
1 cup (250 mL) flour
1 tbsp (15 mL) baking powder
½ tsp (2 mL) salt

1 medium (large) egg
1 cup (250 mL) milk
¼ cup (65 mL) melted butter

Sift together dry ingredients. Beat egg; add milk and butter and pour into dry ingredients, stirring just to moisten. Pour into greased 8 x 8 in. (20 x 20 cm) pan. Bake in 400° oven for 30 minutes. Serve with maple syrup.

EMILY'S DATE AND PINEAPPLE BREAD

¾ cup (175 mL) dates, cut in quarters
1½ tsp (7 mL) soda
1 large (extra-large) egg, well beaten
½ cup (125 mL) brown sugar, not packed
¼ cup (60 mL) white sugar
2 tbsp (30 mL) shortening, melted
½ tsp (2 mL) vanilla extract

½ tsp (2 mL) salt
¾ cup (175 mL) crushed pineapple, undrained
½ banana, mashed
1¼ cup (300 mL) sifted flour
1 cup (250 mL) bran
½ cup (125 mL) chopped nuts
½ cup (125 mL) boiling water

Pour boiling water over dates; stir in soda and set aside till cool. Combine eggs, sugars, shortening, salt, and vanilla. Stir into date mixture. Add remaining ingredients, mixing only till they are just combined. Place in small, greased loaf pan. Bake 1 hour in 300° oven. Turn out and cool. Do not slice until next day as loaf is sticky at first.

PABLUM BROWN BREAD

2 cups (500 mL) "Mixed Cereal" Pablum
1 cup (250 mL) molasses
2 cups (500 mL) buttermilk
1 cup (250 mL) flour
1 cup (250 mL) cornmeal

2 tsp (15 mL) baking soda
1 tsp (7 mL) baking powder
1 tsp (5 mL heaped) salt
1 cup (250 mL) raisins

Sift flour, baking powder, soda, and salt together. Add cornmeal and pablum. Mix buttermilk and molasses together, and combine with dry ingredients. Add raisins. Fill three greased 1 lb (500 g) coffee cans about two-thirds full. Cover with foil, tying tightly. Steam 2 hours.

PABLUM NUT BREAD

NOV 26 '85

1½ cups (375 mL) "Mixed Cereal" Pablum
2 cups (500 mL) flour
2 tbsp (30 mL) baking powder
2 tsp (10 mL) salt

½ cup (125 mL) sugar
2 cups (500 mL) milk
1½ cups (375 mL) chopped nuts

Sift flour, baking powder, salt, and sugar together. Add Pablum to milk. Sift in other dry ingredients. Mix, and pour into well-greased loaf pan. Allow to set for 20 minutes before baking. Bake 1 hour at 375°.

THREE FRUIT BREAD

2 cups (500 mL) flour
4 tsp (20 mL) baking powder
¼ tsp (1 mL) salt
¼ cup (65 mL) solid shortening
1 egg
½ cup (125 mL) sugar

⅓ cup (85 mL) chopped glacé cherries
2 tbsp (30 mL) melted shortening
2 tsp (10 mL) grated orange rind
½ cup (125 mL) crushed pineapple, undrained
⅓ cup (85 mL) orange juice

Combine flour, baking powder, salt, and sugar. Cut in the solid shortening. Add the cherries. Combine egg, melted shortening, orange rind, juice, and pineapple; stir into dry ingredients mixing only enough to moisten all the flour. Place in a greased 8 x 4 in. (20 x 10 cm) loaf pan and bake for 45-50 minutes at 375°F. Cool and remove from pan. This loaf slices better the next day.

PABLUM MUFFINS

1 egg
¾ cup (180 mL) flour
1½ cups (360 mL) "Mixed Cereal"
    Pablum
1 cup (240 mL) milk
¼ tsp (1 mL) soda

2 tsp (10 mL) baking powder
1 tbsp (15 mL) sugar
1 tbsp (15 mL) corn syrup
½ tsp (2 mL) salt
2 tbsp (30 mL) butter
½ cup (120 mL) chopped dates

Sift together flour, baking powder, soda, and salt. Mix in Pablum. Set aside. Cream together sugar, butter, and corn syrup. Beat the egg in the milk and add to creamed mixture, alternately, with Pablum mixture. Fold in dates. Grease medium-sized muffin tins well, or line with paper baking cups, and fill two-thirds full. Bake at 375° for 25 minutes. Make 16-18 muffins.

CUMBERLAND COUNTY BLUEBERRY MUFFINS

2½ cups (625 mL) flour
2½ tsp (13 mL scant) baking powder
¼ tsp (1 mL) salt
½ cup (125 mL) sugar
2 large (extra-large) eggs, lightly
    beaten

½ cup (125 mL) melted butter
1-1½ cup (250-375 mL) fresh
    blueberries, washed
1 cup (250 mL) buttermilk

Mix flour, baking powder, salt, and sugar. Combine buttermilk, eggs, and melted butter. Add all at once to dry ingredients; stir only till all are moistened. Fold in blueberries. Spoon into paper-lined muffin tins filling two-thirds full. Bake 20-25 minutes in 400° oven. Makes approximately 1½ dozen medium-sized muffins.

BAKING POWDER BISCUITS

2 cups (500 mL) flour
4 tsp (20 mL) baking powder
½ tsp (2 mL) salt
5 tbsp (80 mL) butter, or, shortening
¾ cup (185 mL) whole milk

NOV 26 '85

Combine flour, baking powder, and salt in bowl. Cut butter or shortening into flour till it is very finely divided and resembles cornmeal. Add the milk slowly, and use a table knife to mix as this will not push air out of the dough. Turn dough out on a lightly floured board. Too much flour on the board will toughen the biscuits. Pat the dough out flat, about ½ in. (1 cm) thick, fold it over twice and roll out lightly to 1 in. (2.5 cm) thick. Cut the biscuits with a floured cutter and do not cut them too large. Place in greased and floured baking pan. Bake 15-17 minutes in a 450° oven. Serve very hot. Makes about 1 dozen.

WHOLE WHEAT BISCUITS

1 cup (250 mL) white flour
1 cup (250 mL) whole wheat flour
5 tsp (25 mL) baking powder
1 tbsp (15 mL) sugar
4 tbsp (65 mL) shortening, or, butter
¾ cup (185 mL) whole milk

Combine dry ingredients in a bowl. Cut in shortening till mixture resembles cornmeal. Add milk, mixing with knife blade. Turn out on lightly floured board and knead 10 turns. Pat out 1 in. (2.5 cm) thick. Cut out with floured cutter and put on greased cookie sheet. Bake 12-15 minutes in 450° oven. Serve hot.

OATMEAL BISCUITS

1¾ cup (420 mL) white flour
¼ cup (60 mL) oatmeal —
   not rolled oats
¼ tsp (1 mL) salt

1 tsp (5 mL) baking soda
2 tsp (10 mL) cream of tartar
4 tbsp (60 mL) butter
½ cup and 2 tbsp (150 mL) whole milk

Combine flour, oatmeal, salt, soda, and cream of tartar in bowl. Cut in the butter until mixture is like meal. Mix in the milk with a knife blade. Turn out on a lightly floured board. Pat out ½ in. (1 cm) thick. Cut with floured cutter and put on greased baking sheet. Bake 12-15 minutes in 450° oven. Serve at once.

STRAWBERRY SHORTCAKE

2 cups (480 mL) flour
4 tsp (20 mL) baking powder
½ tsp (2 mL) salt
6 tbsp (90 mL) butter
⅔ cup (160 mL) light cream
1 tbsp (15 mL) sugar

Combine dry ingredients in bowl and cut in butter till mixture resembles cornmeal. Add cream to make a soft dough. Pat out ½ in. (1 cm) thick. Fold over and roll out lightly to ¾ in. (2 cm) thickness. Cut with a 3 in. (7.5 cm) cutter and place on greased cookie sheet. Brush with a little milk and sprinkle, very lightly, with granulated sugar. Bake at 450° for 12-15 minutes. Remove from oven. Cool on rack, split and fill with Strawberry Filling. Makes ½ dozen.

STRAWBERRY FILLING

2 cups (500 mL) strawberries
¼-⅓ cup (60-80 mL) sugar
½ pt (200 mL) whipping cream
several whole berries for garnish

Slice strawberries and add sugar to get desired sweetness. Whip cream. Spread split shortcake with a little whipped cream and fill generously with berries. Place a spoonful of berries on top, add a large dollop of whipped cream and place a whole perfect berry on top.

STEAMED DUMPLINGS

2 cups (500 mL) flour
½ tsp (2 mL) salt
4 tsp (20 mL) baking powder
1 cup (250 mL) milk, more or less
2 tsp (10 mL) shortening

Sift the flour with the salt and baking powder. Cut in the shortening until it is very fine. Add sufficient milk to make a very soft dough which will drop off a spoon.

Dumplings to serve with a meat or chicken stew, or a boiled dinner can be cooked in a steamer over boiling water; but they are better if placed right in the stew pot, resting on solid meat or vegetable — not floating on the liquid. Cover the pot very tightly and cook 15 minutes. Do not peek. Trust the dumplings — if they have plenty of steam they will be light and feathery. A pinch of savory or other herbs may be added to the dumpling batter for extra flavour.

PANCAKES

2 cups (500 mL) flour — half of the
  white flour may be replaced with
  whole wheat
3½ tsp (17 mL) baking powder
½ tsp (2 mL) salt
1¾ cups (450 mL) milk
1 small (large) egg
3 tbsp (50 mL) shortening, melted

Sift flour, baking powder, and salt together into a bowl, preferably one with a lip for pouring. Beat the egg till light; add milk and shortening. Mix the liquid with the dry ingredients, and be sure all lumps have disappeared. Heat a griddle or frying pan until quite hot; grease lightly and pour on the batter in spoonfuls. Little pancakes, the size of a silver dollar are delightful to eat — each one a single bite. Leave until bubbles appear and break on the surface, turn and brown on the other side. Serve on a very hot dish as sudden cooling on a cold plate makes them heavy. Serve with melted butter and maple syrup, or thinned warm marmalade.

BUCKWHEAT CAKES

2 cups (500 mL) milk
½ cup (125 mL) cornmeal
½ cup (125 mL) white flour
1 cup (250 mL) buckwheat flour

½ package yeast
¼ cup (50 mL) lukewarm water
1 tsp (5 mL) sugar
¼ tsp (1 mL) soda

Proof the yeast in the lukewarm water with the sugar. Bring the milk just to the boil and pour over the cornmeal. Let stand till lukewarm, and add the white flour, buckwheat flour, and yeast. Let stand overnight, covered. In the morning, stir down and beat in the soda. Fry in a hot, greased pan.

BREWIS

2 cups (500 mL) dry, brown bread cubes
1 cup (250 mL) dry, white bread cubes
¼ cup (65 mL) butter
milk
pinch of nutmeg

Mix bread with butter. Add milk to cover and cook in the top of a double boiler until the bread has absorbed the milk. Add nutmeg and serve with a little molasses or honey poured over.

PORRIDGE

4 cups (1 L) water
1 cup (250 mL) oatmeal — not rolled oats
1 tsp (5 mL) salt

In the top of a double boiler, over direct heat, bring water and salt to a boil. Place over boiling water and cook for at least 1 hour. Note: A crock pot makes great porridge. Use 1¼ cup (310 mL) of oatmeal and cook overnight on *low* setting.

COMPANY MACARONI

1½ cups (375 mL) scalded milk
¼ cup (65 mL) melted butter
3 eggs, well beaten
1 cup (250 mL) cooked macaroni
1 tbsp (15 mL) chopped onion

½ tbsp (7 mL) salt
1 cup (250 mL) soft bread crumbs
½ cup (125 mL) grated mild Cheddar
  cheese
½ cup (125 mL) sliced mushrooms

Combine ingredients in order, reserving ½ cup (125 mL) crumbs. Place in greased casserole and sprinkle top with reserved crumbs. Place in pan of hot water and bake 40 minutes in 350° oven.

MACARONI AND CHEESE

1 heaping cup (250 mL) macaroni
4 tbsp (65 mL) butter
4 tbsp (65 mL) flour
1 tsp (5 mL) salt
pinch of white pepper
2 tsp (10 mL) onion juice

2 cups (500 mL) milk, or, light cream
1 tbsp (15 mL) minced parsley
1 cup (250 mL) grated sharp Cheddar
  cheese
½ cup (125 mL) buttered bread crumbs

If necessary, break macaroni in 1 in. (2.5 cm) pieces. Boil in salted water according to package directions until tender. Drain; pour cold water over; drain again. Melt butter in saucepan; add flour, and stir until bubbly. Cook slowly and carefully for 15 minutes, not letting flour brown. Add salt, pepper, onion juice, and milk, stirring constantly. Cook, stirring, until sauce is thick. Stir in parsley. In a greased casserole, place a layer of macaroni; cover with a layer of cheese; then put a layer of sauce. Continue till ingredients are used up, ending with a layer of sauce. Spread the crumbs over the top and sprinkle a little extra cheese on top. Bake 25 minutes in 375° oven.

Soups, Vegetables, and Salad Dressings

CHICKEN SOUP

stock from boiled fowl
bones of fowl
1 onion
2 sticks celery, if available
3 tbsp (50 mL) rice, washed
savory, salt, pepper

Obtain the stock for this recipe by preparing Boiled Stuffed Fowl — see page 131. After the fowl has been served and the carcass becomes available, chicken soup may be made, using the bones.

Skim the fat from all the reserved stock; add the bones from the fowl, and simmer until the stock is reduced by one third. Heat 1 tbsp (15 mL) of chicken fat or butter, and sauté chopped onion and celery, covered, for 10 minutes. Strain stock into pot and bring to boil. Add rice and pinch of savory. Simmer till rice is tender; season, and serve.

CREAM OF CHICKEN SOUP

stock from boiled fowl
bones of fowl
2 onions
1 cup (250 mL) white meat, chopped
  very fine

3 hard-boiled egg yolks
½ cup (125 mL) fine bread crumbs
2 cups (500 mL) light, 10%, cream
salt, white pepper, celery salt

Refer to the introductory remarks under Chicken Soup.
Add the bones to all the reserved stock, together with 2 onions, peeled and quartered. Simmer until stock is reduced by half. Strain, chill, and skim off all fat. Rub egg yolks through sieve, add crumbs, and chopped chicken meat. Scald cream and pour into mixture slowly. Strain hot chicken broth into cream and keep hot just below the boiling point for 5 minutes. Season with salt, pepper and celery salt. If not quite thick enough add extra bread crumbs or a little mashed potato.

CLAM CHOWDER

2 cups (500 mL) shucked clams
2 oz (50 g) salt pork
1 medium onion, diced
2 large potatoes, peeled and diced
¼ cup (65 mL) chopped celery

1½ tsp (7 mL) salt
  pinch of white pepper
4 large tomatoes, peeled, seeded,
  chopped
clam juice

Sauté the salt pork until golden and fat is rendered. Discard crisp bits. Sauté the onion in the fat until golden. Add potatoes and celery; cover, and cook 10 minutes. Add tomatoes. Measure clam juice and add boiling water to make up to 3 cups (750 mL). Add to vegetables. Cover, simmer 10 minutes more. Meanwhile cut black ends off clams. Cut tough "straps" finely and leave soft part whole. Add to chowder and simmer 5-10 minutes more. Do not overcook clams. Season and serve.

CULLENSKINK

1 lb (500 g) finnan haddie
1 medium onion, minced
2 cups (500 mL) boiling water
1 cup (250 mL) mashed potatoes

2 cups (500 mL) hot milk
salt and pepper
butter

Skin the fish if necessary. Put in saucepan with onion and water and simmer till fish is tender — 5-10 minutes. Remove the fish and separate bones and flesh. Put bones back in broth, cover and cook 1 hour. Strain. Blend in mashed potatoes. Bring to a boil, stirring; add milk, flaked fish, and seasoning. Pour into bowls and put ½ tsp (2 mL) butter on top of each bowl.

LOBSTER STEW

2 boiled lobsters about ¾ lb (375 g) each
1 qt (1 L) whole milk
3 soda crackers
¼ cup (65 mL) butter

1 tsp (5 mL) salt
½ tsp (2 mL) white pepper
5 drops tabasco, or, Outerbridges Sherry Peppers

Remove the meat from the tail and claws of the lobster. Cut the tail meat into ½ in. (1 cm) slices. Pull the hard white "fin" out of the claws, keeping the claws whole if possible. Set aside claws. Set aside 4 pats of butter from the total amount and melt the rest in a large saucepan. Roll the crackers into a fine powder and mix into the melted butter. If you like the "tomalley" — the green liver in the body of the lobster — you can work this in as well but the stew will not have as good a colour. Scald the milk, and add it slowly to the butter paste. Add the lobster meat and, stirring continually, bring the soup almost to the boil. Season with salt and peppers. Ladle into four bowls, putting one claw in each bowl and floating a pat of butter on top of each.

MARY QUEEN OF SCOTS SOUP

2 cups (500 mL) sorrel leaves
2 tbsp (30 mL) butter
1 qt (1 L) white stock
1 large potato, grated

1 tsp (5 mL) salt
½ cup (125 mL) light cream
dash of white pepper

Wash sorrel and remove any tough stalks. Place in saucepan with melted butter and simmer covered for 5-10 minutes, or till all the leaves are wilted. Add the stock, potato, and salt. Simmer 1 hour and then rub through a sieve or whirl in the blender. Reheat and add the cream; heat, but do not allow to boil. Check seasoning, and add a dash of white pepper.

OYSTER STEW

1 cup (250 mL) shelled drained oysters
1 tbsp (15 mL) chopped green onions
juice from the oysters plus milk to equal 1 cup (250 mL)
2 cups (500 mL) light cream
paprika
2 tsp (10 mL) butter

Melt the butter in saucepan and sauté the chopped spring onions, but do not brown. Add oysters and oyster juice together with milk. Simmer gently 10 minutes or till the edges frill. Scald cream and add; season with paprika.

PEA SOUP

6 oz (165 g) split green peas
1 carrot
1 onion
1 potato

1 qt (1 L) water
1 ham bone
½ cup (125 mL) milk

Peel and finely chop the carrot, onion, and potato. Put in pan with peas, ham bone, and water. Cook for 2 hours or until peas are soft, stirring from time to time. Remove ham bone; put mixture through sieve. Add milk and season to taste. Heat to boiling point and serve.

SCOTCH BROTH

1 lb (500 g) lean stewing beef, or,
    mutton
meat bones
1 leek, chopped
3 carrots, diced
1 very small turnip, diced

1½ qt (1.5 L) cold water
⅓ cup (85 mL) pearl barley
¼ cup (65 mL) soaked dried peas
salt and pepper
½ cup (125 mL) chopped spinach
2 tbsp (30 mL) chopped parsley

Dice the meat. Put meat, peas, barley, and water into pan with any bones. Bring to boil and skim. Add the vegetables and simmer 3-4 hours. Remove the bones; remove excess fat. Add spinach and parsley. Cook 10 minutes; season and serve.

SHEEP'S HEAD BROTH

1 lamb's head, split
1 cup (250 mL) diced carrot
1 cup (250 mL) diced turnip
1 cup (250 mL) diced celery
1 cup (250 mL) chopped onion

⅓ cup (85 mL) pearl barley
1½ qt (1.5 L) water
salt and pepper
2 tbsp (30 ml) chopped parsley

Wash the head and soak overnight. Remove the brains and set aside. Put the head, barley, 1 tsp (5 mL) salt, and ¼ tsp (1 mL) pepper, with enough water to cover, in a kettle. Boil, skim, and simmer for 1½ hours. Add the vegetables and cook 1½ hours longer. Remove the head. Slice the meat from the head. Remove the tongue, skin it, and dice the meat. Add the meats to the soup. Taste for seasoning. Garnish with parsley.
Note: The brains may be washed and sprinkled with vinegar, simmered for 10 minutes in water to cover, drained, and chopped. The chopped brains may be added to the soup.

TOMATO SOUP

6 very ripe tomatoes	1 tsp (5 mL) sugar
2 tsp (10 mL) butter	1 qt (1 L) veal stock, or, chicken stock
6 green onions	1 tbsp (15 mL) lemon juice
1 tsp (5 mL) salt	2 tbsp (30 mL) chopped parsley

Peel, seed, and chop tomatoes. Melt butter in soup kettle. Chop onions finely and add to butter. Cover and cook gently for 5 minutes. Add tomatoes and cook covered for 15 minutes more. Add stock, salt, and sugar; simmer 20 minutes uncovered. Add lemon juice; check seasoning; add parsley. Serve.

VEGETABLE SOUP

2 onions, finely chopped	2 tbsp (30 mL) drippings, or, butter
2 carrots, thinly sliced	salt
1 parsnip, thinly sliced	pepper
½ small turnip, diced	1 tbsp (15 mL) chopped parsley
2 potatoes, diced	2 qt (2 L) stock, or, water

Put butter in soup kettle over medium heat; add onions. Cover and cook 5 minutes. Add rest of vegetables, except potatoes; cover, and cook on low for 15 minutes. Add stock and simmer 2 hours. Add potatoes and parsley. Cook 20 minutes more, or till potato cubes are tender. Season.

WEED SOUP

2 qt (2 L) pigweed or lamb's quarters greens
1 cup (250 mL) diced salt pork
1 onion, chopped fine
2 potatoes, peeled and diced
½ cup (125 mL) oatmeal — not rolled oats
salt and pepper

Use just the tips of the pigweed stalks. Wash and discard any tough stalks. Place in a large kettle and add about 4 qt (4 L) boiling water. Boil uncovered for 3 minutes; then drain and chop coarsely. In saucepan, cook pork until crisp. Add the onion and cook until golden — about 15 minutes. Add 5 cups of water; bring to a boil and add potato and chopped pigweed. Bring to a boil and stir in oatmeal. Simmer ½-¾ of an hour, stirring frequently. Season with salt and pepper. Soup should be quite thick.

ASPARAGUS TIPS

1 lb (500 g) young asparagus
2 tbsp (30 mL) melted butter
pepper and salt

Break off the tough ends of asparagus stalks. Take off scales and wash stalks very well. Separate into four bunches and tie them loosely with string. Stand stalks upright, tips uppermost, in the bottom of a double boiler; invert the top half of the double boiler over the asparagus or cover with a cone of foil. Cook in boiling, salted water for 15 minutes or till tender. Do not overcook. Drain; cut off string; drizzle with melted butter; season with salt and pepper.

BAKED BEANS

3 cups (750 mL) dried beans —
  yellow-eyed if available
2 qt (2.5 L) water
¼ tsp (1 mL) soda
2 tsp (10 mL) salt
½ tsp (2 mL) dry mustard

1 tbsp (15 mL) onion, finely chopped
¼ tsp (1 mL) paprika
2 tbsp (30 mL) brown sugar
½ cup (125 mL) molasses
½ lb (250 g) salt pork, cut in three
  pieces

Put beans to soak overnight in cold water. Next morning, drain; cover with fresh water; bring to the boil; add soda; and simmer, covered, until beans are soft when pinched. DO NOT LET BEANS BOIL. Drain; place one piece of salt pork on the bottom of the bean crock. Pour in half the beans; put in another piece of pork; pour in remainder of beans, and top with last piece of pork. Combine salt, mustard, onion, paprika, sugar, molasses, and ½ cup (125 mL) boiling water. Mix well and pour over beans, lifting beans carefully with a spoon so seasoning will go to the bottom of the pot. If liquid does not reach the top of beans, add more water but do not drown the beans. Cover and bake 6 hours in 300° oven, adding a little water if necessary. Uncover during last hour to brown the pork.

BEETS IN ORANGE SAUCE

½ tbsp (7 mL) cornstarch
1 tbsp (15 mL) cold water
2 tbsp (30 mL) grated orange peel
2 tbsp (30 mL) lemon juice

½ cup (125 mL) orange juice
¼ cup (65 mL) butter
3 cups (750 mL) cooked beets
1 hard-boiled egg yolk

Mix the cornstarch and water, stirring to blend without lumps. Add peel, orange, and lemon juices. Cook till clear and thick. Add butter and beets and heat through. Place in serving dish and sprinkle with grated egg yolk.

CLAPSHOT

1 cup (250 mL) mashed potatoes
1 cup (250 mL) mashed turnips
¼ cup (60 mL) hot milk
salt and pepper to taste

Combine all ingredients. If the turnips or potatoes are leftovers, heat the mixture over boiling water. When hot, stir in 1 tbsp (15 mL) butter.

CORN ON THE COB

1 dozen corn, freshly picked
1 pat of butter per person

Shuck the corn immediately before cooking. In a large kettle, boil enough unsalted water to cover the corn. When the water is boiling hard, drop the corn into the water, return to the boil and, at once, turn off the heat. Cover, and let stand 10 minutes before serving. Wrap each pat of butter in a little square of surgical gauze. Give one to each person to rub over the corn before eating. Season with salt and pepper.

BUTTERED PARSNIPS

8 parsnips
2 tbsp (30 mL) butter
½ tsp (2 mL) salt
1 tsp (5 mL) pepper
¼ cup (50 mL) flour

Wash the parsnips; scrape. Cover with boiling water and boil, uncovered, for 30 minutes, or until tender. Be careful not to overcook parsnips. Slice lengthwise ¼ in. (0.5 cm) thick. Combine flour and seasonings; roll the parsnips in seasoned flour, and sauté in melted butter.

DANDELION GREENS

1 qt (1 L) young dandelion leaves
¼ cup (60 mL) butter
1 tsp (5 mL) salt
few drops vinegar

Wash leaves well but do not dry. Melt 1 tbsp (15 ml) of butter in saucepan and place wet greens in saucepan with the salt. Cover and cook gently for 15 minutes. Drain carefully and place in heated serving dish. Drizzle the rest of the butter over, and sprinkle with vinegar.

FIDDLEHEADS

2 cups (500 mL) fiddleheads
1 cup (250 mL) boiling water
1 tsp (5 mL) salt
2 tbsp (30 mL) butter
1 tbsp (15 mL) lemon juice

Wash and clean the fiddleheads, pulling off the brown bracket at the base if still adhering. Put them in a saucepan with boiling water and salt, and cover. Cook gently for 15 minutes. Drain; return to saucepan in which butter has been melted and heated to bubbling. Toss to coat all over and, when very hot, sprinkle with lemon juice and serve.

HODGEPODGE

¼ lb (100 g) salt pork, cut in strips
new potatoes — red jackets if possible
new peas
3-4 green onions, chopped with some of the green
baby carrots
new string beans
½ cup (125 mL) cream

Scrub potatoes, but do not peel. Shell peas. Cut beans in 2 in. (5 cm) lengths; scrub carrots. The potatoes, beans, and carrots can be boiled in one pot. Cook the peas separately. Do not overcook and use a minimum of water. Drain the vegetables and save the water in which they were boiled. Fry the salt pork until it is crisp and brown. Remove the pork and sauté the chopped onion. Add ½ cup (125 mL) of the vegetable water and the cream. Bring to a boil and add cooked vegetables and pork to the pan. Serve when piping hot.

BAKED MUSHROOMS

1 qt (1 L) mushrooms
¼ cup (65 mL) butter
1 tbsp (15 mL) lemon juice
½ cup (125 mL) bread crumbs
salt and pepper

Wipe mushrooms; remove stalks and use for some other purpose. Grease a 1 qt (1 L) casserole. Arrange a layer of mushroom caps, gill side down. Sprinkle with salt, pepper, lemon juice, and bread crumbs. Dot well with butter. Repeat until all mushrooms are used, ending with bread crumbs. Cover with a buttered sheet of any kind of light paper — parchment is best, if obtainable — and bake in 350° oven for 20 minutes.

HOT MUSHROOM SANDWICH

Ingredients per Sandwich:
2 slices whole wheat bread, toasted
6-8 field mushrooms, cleaned
2 tsp (10 mL) butter

¼ tsp (1 mL) lemon juice
pinch of pepper
½ tsp (2 mL) chopped parsley
butter

Stem the mushrooms; chop the stems and sauté in a little butter. Combine 2 tsp (10 mL) butter with lemon juice, pepper, and chopped parsley. Spread slices of toast with butter mixture. On one slice of toast sprinkle sautéed mushroom stems; top with mushroom caps, gill side down. Brush with a little melted butter and bake in a covered dish in 350° oven for 12-15 minutes. Top with other toast slice which has been kept warm; alternatively, sandwich may be served without top.

SAUTEED PUFFBALLS

puffballs — should be white right through
lemon juice
fine dry bread crumbs
¼ cup (65 mL) butter

Wash puffballs and slice into rounds about ½ in. (1 cm) thick. Sprinkle well with lemon juice and water, and coat with crumbs. Melt butter in skillet and sauté the puffball slices over medium heat until golden.

GOLDILOCKS POTATOES

2½ cups (625 mL) hot mashed potatoes
salt and pepper
½ cup (125 mL) heavy cream
6 tbsp (90 mL) grated mild cheese
hot milk

Be sure the potatoes are light and dry. Season with salt and pepper. Beat in hot milk until the potatoes are whipped light. The amount will vary. Place in greased custard cups. Whip the cream and fold in cheese. Spread over potatoes and bake in 350° oven for 15 minutes.

NEW POTATOES WITH MINT

new potatoes — golf ball size
2 large sprigs of mint
1 tsp (5 mL) salt
butter
1 tsp (5 mL) finely chopped mint leaves

Allow 4-5 potatoes per serving. Scrub potatoes and place in saucepan with the sprigs of mint. Cover with boiling salted water and cook till potatoes are tender. Drain; discard mint. Slip skins off potatoes. Melt a little butter in frying pan and toss potatoes in it; do not let them colour. Sprinkle with chopped mint leaves.

WINTER POTATO SALAD

3 cups (750 mL) cubed, cooked potatoes
3 hard-boiled egg yolks
1 small onion
1 tsp (5 mL) celery seed
¾ cup (185 mL) cooked salad dressing
salt, pepper, paprika, parsley

Slice onion and sprinkle with salt. Let stand ½ hour. Boil potatoes until just done — do not overcook — and dice while hot. Keep them warm while mixing, for better appearance and flavour. Squeeze the onions to get rid of strong juice; then cut up to make 1 tbsp (15mL) of finely chopped onion. Mix potatoes, onion, celery seed, and grated egg yolk, reserving 1 tbsp (15 mL) egg yolk for garnish. Toss with salad dressing and season. Chill; garnish with paprika, grated egg, and chopped parsley if available.

SCALLOPED POTATOES

4 medium potatoes, peeled
½ tsp (2 mL) salt
1½ tbsp (25 mL) flour
2 cups (525 mL) milk
1 tbsp (15 mL) butter
fresh ground pepper

Slice potatoes thin. In a greased baking dish, place a layer of potato slices. Sprinkle with salt, pepper, and flour. Add another layer of potatoes. Sprinkle again. Continue until all potatoes are used. Pour in milk. Dot with butter and bake 1½ hours in a 350° oven.

STOVIES

4 medium potatoes, peeled
1-2 onions
salt and pepper
1 tbsp (15 mL) butter
1 cup (250 mL) chicken stock
¼ cup (65 mL) chopped parsley

Slice potatoes thinly, and slice onions crosswise in thin slices. Grease a heavy frying pan with a cover. Place a layer of potatoes and sprinkle with salt and pepper; repeat with another layer of seasoned potatoes, and then a layer of onions, sprinkled with parsley. Continue till all potatoes and onions are used up. For best appearance, top layer should be potatoes, Pour in chicken stock; cover and simmer 1 hour, or until potatoes are tender.

BROWNED RICE

1 cup (250 mL) long grained rice
1 tbsp (15 mL) minced onion
2 tsp (10 mL) butter
1 tsp (5 mL) salt

Wash rice by shaking in a sieve under cold running water then let it stand in cold water for 20 minutes. Melt butter in a saucepan with cover and sauté onion in it until the onion is limp. Drain the rice and add it to saucepan. Cook, uncovered, until the water still clinging to the rice has evaporated, and the rice is beginning to brown. Add 1½ cups boiling water and salt, and cook covered on low heat for 20 minutes. Do not uncover during this cooking time. Stir with a fork and serve.

SAUERKRAUT

10 lb (5 kg) cabbage
¼ lb (125 g) coarse salt

To ferment the sauerkraut you will need a large earthenware crock with a round board, cut to fit the inside circumference. The board should fit well but be able to slide up and down freely inside the crock. Pull the coarse outside leaves off the cabbage, plus any leaves that are damaged or withered. Shred the cabbage; wash, and drain it. Arrange the cabbage in layers, sprinkling each layer with salt and tapping it down well with a heavy potato masher. When all the cabbage is used up, lay a clean cloth on the surface; place the wooden board on top and weight it with a heavy, smooth stone. Do not use metal weights or bricks. Leave. On the following day, water will rise above the board. The fermentation will cause a froth to form. At the end of about 3 weeks, fermentation ceases and the sauerkraut is ready. Remove desired amount; wash, and use as needed. Each time replace the board and weight, but remove a little of the liquid. Do not let any metal come in contact with the sauerkraut.

BAKED SQUASH

acorn squash, or, winter squash
melted butter
salt, pepper, and sugar

Halve squash; remove seeds and stringy portion. Pare the winter squash and cut in serving pieces; acorn squash may be left in halves, with the skin on. Place in a shallow baking dish; brush with melted butter; sprinkle with salt, pepper, and sugar. Add hot water to cover the bottom of baking dish if using acorn squash; leave winter squash dry. Cover. Bake 45-60 minutes in 400° oven, or until tender. If desired, cooked squash may be mashed and is much drier than when it is boiled.

STUFFED SQUASH

4 acorn squash
4 strips bacon
1 small onion, chopped
1 cup (250 mL) chopped swiss chard,
   or, spinach

1 egg, beaten
1 tsp (5 mL) savory
1 tbsp (15 mL) minced parsley
¾ cup (185 mL) ground lean beef
pepper and salt

Parboil the squash 10 minutes and split lengthwise. Remove seeds and stringy bits. Remove pulp from two halves and chop fine. Fry bacon until crisp; set aside and fry onions in bacon fat until golden. Add chopped greens and pulp, and sauté 7 minutes. Cool; add egg, bacon, beef, and seasonings. Mix well and stuff the remaining squash halves. Place in buttered baking dish and bake 30 minutes in 400° oven.

PUFFY SWEET POTATOES

2 cups (500 mL) cooked, drained, and mashed sweet potato
2 tbsp (30 mL) melted butter
¼ cup (60 mL) milk
1 egg, beaten
salt and pepper

Combine all ingredients and beat till fluffy. Drop big spoonfuls on a greased cookie sheet. Place in 375° oven and cook till puffed and golden.

BOILED DRESSING

1 tbsp (15 mL) flour
½ tsp (2 mL) salt
1 tsp (5 mL) mustard
dash of cayenne

1 whole egg, or, 2 egg yolks
½ cup (125 mL) milk
¼ cup (65 mL) vinegar
1 tbsp (15 mL) butter

Combine the dry ingredients in the top of a double boiler and add the beaten egg. Add the milk gradually and, stirring constantly, cook over hot water until the mixture thickens. Slowly add the vinegar; remove from heat and add the butter. If this is to be used as a dressing for fruit salad, up to 3 tsp (15 mL) of sugar may be incorporated.

FRUIT SALAD DRESSING

2 egg yolks
pinch of salt
⅓ cup (75 mL) sugar
¼ cup (55 mL) pineapple syrup,
  drained from tin

¼ cup (55 mL) orange juice, heated
2 tbsp (30 mL) lemon juice, heated
2 egg whites

Beat the egg yolks; add the salt and half the sugar. Gradually pour in the heated fruit juices. Cook over hot water, stirring till thick. Beat the egg whites stiff with the remaining sugar and fold into cooked mixture. Chill and serve with fruit salad.

Fish and Seafood

SALT COD

To precook salt cod, soak it overnight, skin side up. If soaking in daytime, change water a couple of times. When soaked, cover with fresh water and heat, just below simmering point, until cod is soft. Remove skin and bones, and flake. Use in recipes.

CODFISH BALLS

1 cup (250 mL) salt codfish, flaked
3½ cups (825 mL) potatoes, boiled, diced
2 eggs
1 tbsp (15 mL) butter
flour, salt, and pepper

Mix flaked codfish with hot potatoes. Mash together. Beat eggs; add to potato mixture with butter. Add salt and pepper to taste. Shape into patties and flour lightly. Fry in bacon fat or rendered salt pork.

COD 'N' CABBAGE

1 lb (500 g) salt cod
2 onions, chopped
3 tomatoes — fresh or canned —
    peeled, seeded, chopped

5 cups (1250 mL) shredded cabbage
½ cup (125 mL) water
1 tbsp (15 mL) vinegar
small piece salt pork

Soak, skin, and bone cod but do not precook. Cut in chunks. Render the salt pork in a skillet, or use oil. Sauté onion till golden; add cabbage, tomatoes, fish, water, and vinegar. Simmer, covered, for 15 minutes until cabbage is tender.

CREAMED COD

1½ cups (375 mL) white sauce
1½ cups (375 mL) flaked codfish
salt, pepper, and cayenne
toast

Combine White Sauce and fish; season; heat through, and serve on toast.

HOUSE BANKING

1½ lb (750 g) salt cod
4 potatoes, peeled and sliced
4 onions, sliced
2½ cups (625 mL) milk
1 tbsp (15 mL) butter
salt, pepper, and flour

Soak cod but do not precook. Skin, bone, and cut in small pieces. Grease a casserole, and layer the cod, onions, and potatoes in that order, sprinkling each layer with a little flour, and seasoning with salt and pepper. End with potatoes. Dot with butter and add milk. Bake 1½ hours in 350° oven.

FRIED SALT COD

1 lb (500 g) salt cod
¼ cup (65 mL) fat
1 onion, chopped
1 tbsp (15 mL) chopped parsley
1 tbsp (15 mL) cream

Soak and precook the cod but do not flake. Heat the fat in skillet and sauté the onion until brown. Add the cod and sauté fish 5 minutes per side until it starts to brown. Remove the cod and set aside. Add 1 tbsp (15 mL) of the liquid cod was cooked in. Deglaze the pan by cooking gently and scraping to remove all brown bits adhering to the bottom of the pan. Blend in cream. Add parsley; heat to the boiling point and pour over fish.

BAKED CLAMS

4 dozen clams in shells
½ cup (125 mL) hot water
1 cup (250 mL) white sauce
1 cup (250 mL) fine dry crumbs
¼ cup (65 mL) melted butter

Scrub the clams in cold, running water to get rid of sand. Put in a big kettle, add water, and boil gently 20 minutes until the shells open. Pour off juice and let it settle; use juice to make sauce. Cut clams in two, if large, and cut off black ends. Mix clams with White Sauce and fill the cleaned shells. Place filled shells in a shallow baking dish. Mix crumbs with melted butter. Sprinkle over shells and bake in 350° oven for 20 minutes or until browned and bubbly. Note: When buying clams, you may find that some have their shells open. Tap them smartly and, if the shells do not close up, discard them for the clams are dead. Also, discard any that do not open after being heated.

FRIED CLAMS

1 pt (500 mL) large clams, drained
1 egg, beaten
1 cup (250 mL) fine, dry bread crumbs

Roll the clams in the crumbs; dip in egg and roll in crumbs again. Fry in shallow fat for 2 or 3 minutes. Drain.

FIDDLEHEADS AND FINNAN HADDIE

2 cups (500 mL) cooked fiddleheads
1 lb piece of finnan haddie — smoked haddock — cooked and flaked
2 cups (500 mL) milk — use milk in which haddock was cooked
4 tbsp (60 mL) butter

3 tbsp (45 mL) flour
salt and pepper
1 tbsp (15 mL) butter
bread crumbs
nutmeg

Melt 4 tbsp (60 mL) butter in saucepan. Add flour and cook for 20 minutes, without letting it brown. Stir in the milk slowly and cook till thickened. Season with salt and pepper and a few grains of nutmeg. Grease an oven-proof casserole and layer the fiddleheads and fish. Pour the white sauce over, sprinkle with bread crumbs, and dot with butter. Bake in 325° oven 20-25 minutes.

FISH PUDDING

3 cups (750 mL) flaked
  cooked haddock
1 onion, chopped
¼ cup (65 mL) butter
2 tbsp (30 mL) flour
2 cups (500 mL) milk

1 tsp (5 mL) salt
¼ cup (65 mL) grated cheese
juice of half a lemon
6 large potatoes, peeled and thinly sliced
2 tbsp (30 mL) fine dry bread crumbs
1 tbsp (15 mL) melted butter

Melt butter in skillet; sauté onion until brown. Stir in flour and cook for 15 minutes. Scald the milk and stir slowly into the flour and butter. Cook until sauce bubbles. Add salt, cheese, and lemon juice. Layer the potatoes and fish and pour sauce over. Cover with crumbs, which have been tossed in the butter. Bake 1 hour in 350° oven.

FRIED HERRING

small herrings — 1 per person
flour
beaten egg
fine dry bread crumbs
lemon wedges
fat for deep frying

Roll the herrings in flour. Dip them in the beaten egg and shake them in a bag full of bread crumbs. Deep fry until golden and crisp. Serve with a wedge of lemon.

SOLOMON GUNDY

6 salt herring
1 large onion, thinly sliced
2 cups (500 mL) vinegar
2 tbsp (30 mL) pickling spice
⅓ cup (85 mL) sugar

Place the fish on a board, backbone upwards. Press hard all along backbone to loosen it. Turn over and starting at the tail pull the backbone out, using a nail file to raise up the bone. Most of the ribs will come out together. Pull off skin. Cut in pieces about 1 in. (2.5 cm) thick. Soak overnight. Layer alternately with onion in bottles. Bring vinegar, pickling spice, and sugar to a boil. Cool and pour over herrings. Let stand overnight before serving.

BOILED LOBSTER

Pick small to medium-sized live lobsters which feel heavy for their size. Do not boil lobsters in straight sea water; it is not salty enough. Add extra salt, about ¼ cup (50 mL) per qt (L) of sea water. If you are using fresh water add the above amount of salt plus a further 1 tsp (5 mL) per qt (L) of water. Have a large kettle of this salted water boiling furiously. Drop the live lobster head first into the water. This ensures that death is instantaneous because the ganglion of the central nervous system is just behind the eyes and, as soon as the hot water touches it, the animal dies. Lobsters do *not* scream when put into boiling water; however, it is cruel to drop them in, any old way, or to put too many in at once, for this lowers the water temperature and they do not die immediately. Unless you have a very big pot, only cook two or three at a time; and put them into the water one at a time. Cover the pot and cook 20 minutes. Remove the lobsters from the hot water and *at once* quench them in cold water to prevent overcooking. Hang them up to drain for a few minutes — you can peg them out on the clothesline. This prevents their soaking up water which softens the meat.

LOBSTER ROLL

meat from 1 small lobster
soft roll
lettuce
mayonnaise, or, salad dressing
salt and pepper

Cut the lobster meat into ¼ in. (0.5) cm) slices. Shred the lettuce; toss the lobster meat and sufficient salad dressing to coat the pieces lightly. Season with salt and pepper. Pile on a long soft roll.

LOBSTER SALAD

1 lobster for every two people
1 boiled potato per person
1 hard-boiled egg per person
boiled salad dressing, or, mayonnaise

salt and pepper
paprika
1 stick celery per person

Remove the meat from the lobster, keeping the claws intact. Set claws aside and chop the rest of the meat into fine dice. Dice the boiled potato and the hard-boiled egg white. Grate the yolk. Chop the celery very fine. Combine all the ingredients in a large bowl; season with salt and pepper. Add enough salad dressing to bind the salad together. Check seasoning. Chill. Using an ice-cream scoop, serve the salad on lettuce leaves; sprinkle with paprika and garnish with whole lobster claw.

SCALLOPED LOBSTER IN BOATS

2 boiled lobsters, weighing 1½ lb (750 g) each
2 tbsp (30 mL) butter
½ cup (125 mL) liquid drained from lobster, or, water
½ cup (125 mL) white wine, or, water

2 tbsp (30 mL) flour
2 tbsp (30 mL) brandy
¼ cup (65 mL) butter
½ pt (200 mL) whipping cream
salt and pepper

Remove the meat from the lobsters, keeping the claws intact, if possible, and carefully removing the meat from the tails so as to keep the red parts, upper sides, of the shells unbroken, with the fans at the end left whole. Cut away the membranes from the sides and wash the shells carefully. Set the shells aside, together with the whole claws. Melt 2 tbsp (30 mL) butter in a heavy saucepan. Add the flour and cook, without browning, till it bubbles and the grains of flour burst; this will take about 20 minutes. Add the lobster juice and wine, bring to a boil, and simmer for 30 minutes. Chop the lobster meat in coarse pieces. Melt the ¼ cup (65 mL) butter and sauté the meat till the skin is dark red. Add brandy, then the white sauce, and mix well. Cook 5 minutes and add the cream. Bring almost to a boil. Put the two tail shells together, end to end, to make a boat shaped container, pushing one into the other. Fill with lobster scallop. Set the "sails" by sticking the whole claws, heated separately, upright at intervals along the boat.

BAKED MACKEREL

1 lb (0.5 kg) whole fish per serving
cooking oil

Wipe mackerel; clean, and brush all over with oil. Wrap fish in foil, and bake 20 minutes in 425° oven. Note: A 4 lb (2 kg) mackerel will serve four people; however, the fish seldom come this big. They are usually 1-2 lb (0.5 - 1 kg) in size.

When buying any fish, allow 1 lb (500 g) whole fish per person; ½ lb (250 g) dressed fish per person; ⅓ lb (175 g) fish fillets per person.

STUFFED BAKED MACKEREL

1 small mackerel or "tinker" per person

Stuffing per Four Mackerel:
1½ cups (375 mL) chopped onion
1 cup (250 mL) soft bread crumbs
½ cup (125 mL) diced celery, or
½ tsp (2 mL) celery salt
3 fresh tomatoes, or 3 canned

tomatoes, drained
6 tbsp (95 mL) butter
salt and pepper
½ tsp (2 mL) thyme
2 tbsp (30 mL) butter

Sauté the onion, celery, and tomatoes in the butter until onion is limp. Add bread crumbs and seasonings. Stuff the cleaned fish and sew up openings. Rub the fish with 2 tbsp (30 mL) butter each. Grease a shallow baking pan or pie plate and place fish in it. Bake 15 minutes in a 425° oven, basting with pan drippings every 5 minutes.

FRIED MACKEREL

1 mackerel per person
oatmeal — not rolled oats
1 tbsp (15 mL) oil
2 tbsp (30 mL) butter

Clean the fish and cut off heads and tails. Roll each fish in oatmeal. Heat oil in heavy skillet. Melt butter in the oil and fry the fish 6 minutes each side.

SOUSED MACKEREL

2-3 small mackerel
1 cup (250 mL) water
3 cups (750 mL) vinegar
¼ cup (65 mL) pickling spice tied in cheesecloth bag
2 tsp (10 mL) salt

Clean mackerel and place in a glass or ceramic ovenproof dish. Pour the rest of ingredients over the fish. Cook 3-4 hours in 275° oven. Let cool in liquid. Serve cold.

OYSTERS ON THE HALF SHELL

oysters
red wine vinegar
pepper

To open oysters, a proper oyster knife is necessary. The hand holding the oyster should be protected with an oven mitt or a heavy leather glove. The oyster has a curved edge and a straight edge. The hinge is at the point of the oyster. Insert the knife between the shells on the curved side about 1 in. (2.5 cm) away from the hinge. Twist the blade to pry the flat shell off. Cut the muscle from its point of attachment and then slip the knife under the oyster to release it from the bottom shell. One shell is deep, one flatter. The flat side is the top side. Serve the oyster in the deep shell. Run the oyster through your fingers to remove any shell chips or pearls but DO NOT WASH OYSTERS; it ruins the flavour. Replace in shell and lay the shell on a bed of crushed ice. Sprinkle with vinegar and pepper. No salt is necessary; oysters are quite salty.

OYSTERS "BAKED" ON THE HALF SHELL

1 dozen oysters
1 hard-boiled egg yolk, grated
1 tbsp (15 mL) chopped parsley
¼ cup (65 mL) melted butter
6 tbsp (100 mL) fine, soft bread crumbs

Open the oysters and leave them in the bottom shell. Sprinkle each with parsley and a little grated egg yolk. Put them in a 250° oven for 10 minutes. Meanwhile, heat the butter in a heavy saucepan until it is a little browned. Add the bread crumbs and fry them in the butter for a few minutes. When crisp and golden, sprinkle over the oysters.

COLD POACHED SALMON

1 whole salmon grilse, weighing 3-4 lb (1.5-2 kg)
½ bottle dry white wine — optional
½ lb (250 g) onions, halved
½ lb (250 g) carrots, scraped and coarsely chopped
½ lb (250 g) celery, coarsely chopped
few sprigs of parsley
salt

Wrap the fish in cheesecloth; place in large roaster or fish poacher and cover with cold water. Add remaining ingredients. Slowly bring to a boil; cover and cook very gently for 10 minutes only! Take off the heat and leave to cool with the lid on. When cold, leave salmon in the juice and refrigerate for up to 2 days, as the salmon will improve in flavour.

SALMON STEAKS

1 salmon steak, 4-6 oz (125-175 g) per person
butter
lemon juice
chopped parsley

Grease a sheet of foil for each steak. Place steak on the centre of each sheet of foil. Top with 1 tsp (5 mL) of butter. Bring edges together and fold over twice. Twist open ends to seal. Place packages on baking sheet and bake 20 minutes in 325° oven. Remove steak onto plate and pour juices over. Sprinkle lemon juice over and sprinkle with chopped parsley.

BAKED SCALLOPS

1 lb (500 g) shucked scallops
6 tbsp (100 mL) butter
1 cup (250 mL) fine dry bread crumbs
1 cup (250 mL) homogenized milk, more or less
1 tbsp (15 mL) chopped parsley
salt and pepper

Grease a shallow casserole and sprinkle with crumbs. Place scallops in a single layer in the dish and sprinkle with salt and pepper. Melt the butter and toss with the remaining bread crumbs and parsley. Pour milk into the dish just until it reaches the top of the scallops but do not let it drown them. Sprinkle the bread crumbs on top and bake in a 325° oven for 35-40 minutes.

FRIED SCALLOPS

1 lb (500 g) big shucked scallops
flour
salt and pepper
2 tbsp (30 mL) oil
¼ cup (60 mL) butter
1 tbsp (15 mL) lemon juice

Mix flour, salt, and pepper and roll the scallops in the seasoned flour until they are well coated. Heat the oil in a skillet until very hot. Reduce the heat and add the butter all at once. As soon as the butter is melted and foamy, add the scallops, six or eight at a time, and sauté quickly. Do not overcook them or they will toughen. Keep warm, and sprinkle with lemon juice. Do not pile them up, while keeping, but put them on greased brown paper in a 250° oven, with a layer of paper over them.

BAKED SHAD

1 shad, weighing 4 lb (2 kg)	pepper
2 cups (450 mL) cooked rice	2 tbsp (30 mL) minced onion
½ tsp (2 mL) ground ginger	1 tbsp (15 mL) lemon juice
salt	oil

Clean the fish and remove as many bones as possible. Sprinkle cavity with salt, pepper, and ground ginger. Combine the rice, onion, and lemon juice and add salt and pepper till mixture is quite sharp. Fill the fish with this mixture; close cavity with skewers and string, or sew it. Brush the fish with oil; sprinkle with salt and pepper and wrap it in greased foil, twisting ends to seal. Bake in 350° oven for 30 minutes. Open foil; sprinkle fish with lemon juice and increase oven to 400°. Bake fish 20 minutes more, basting from time to time.

PANBROILED SHAD

3½-4 lb (1.5-2 kg) shad, filleted
½ cup (125 mL) salad oil
juice of 1 lemon
2 sprigs parsley, chopped

Marinate the fillets for an hour in the mixture of oil, lemon juice, and parsley. Heat a heavy, cast-iron frying pan and panbroil the fish for 5 minutes per side.

FRIED TROUT

1 small trout per person, not larger than 6 oz (175 g)
flour, or, cornmeal
salt and pepper
fresh shortening

Clean the trout, leaving head and tail attached. Salt and pepper the fish, inside and out; roll in flour. Melt the shortening in a heavy skillet. Use sufficient shortening to come two-thirds of the way up the fish. Heat the fat very hot and fry the fish 5 minutes per side. You can now remove backbone, head, and tail in one piece, with the ribs as well. Push the meat off each side; pick up the head and tail and the whole skeleton will come away, leaving the meat on the plate.

SEA TROUT

Sea trout are cooked whole in the same way as salmon but, as they are generally smaller, the simmering time should be reduced to 5 minutes. See Cold Poached Salmon.

FRIED SMELTS

2 lb (1 kg) small smelts
2 eggs
⅓ cup (85 mL) milk
2 tbsp (30 mL) oil

½ tsp (2 mL) salt
¼ tsp (1 mL) pepper
flour
cornmeal

Wash and dry the cleaned smelts. Cut off heads. Combine beaten eggs with next four ingredients. Roll the smelts in flour; dip them in egg mixture; roll in cornmeal. Fry the smelts, four to six at a time, in deep fat 375°F (190°C) for 1-2 minutes. Drain on absorbent paper. Put the smelts on a rack in a pan in a slow oven, 225°, to keep warm while others fry. Serve with lemon wedges.

WHITE SAUCE

¼ cup (65 mL) butter
½ cup (125 mL) flour
2½ cups (625 mL) whole milk
salt and pepper
pinch of nutmeg — optional

Melt the butter but do not let it colour. Add the flour and mix well. Now the flour and butter must cook on low heat for 20 minutes. If it is not cooked sufficiently, the sauce will be heavy, tasting of uncooked flour. It is important not to let it take on colour, so a very heavy saucepan is important. Add the milk slowly and stir constantly until it thickens. Simmer for a few minutes, adding a little more milk if it seems too thick. Add salt, white pepper, and nutmeg.

Meat, Poultry, and Game

ROAST BEEF

5-6 lb (2.5-3 kg) roast of beef
extra beef suet, if necessary
salt, pepper, and flour
4-5 potatoes, peeled and quartered

Leave the bone in roast beef for best flavour. Wipe meat; season with salt and pepper, and flour lightly. If the roast is very lean, tie a piece of suet over it. Place a couple of small, walnut-sized pieces of suet in the pan. Place roast on small rack, or use bones as rack in rib roast. Do not let rack cover whole bottom of roaster. Place meat in 500° oven and leave until all sides are browned. Baste with fat often. When all sides are browned, reduce heat to 325°; add the potatoes to the pan and turn them to coat with pan dripping. Continue roasting until meat reaches 130° on meat thermometer for rare; 140° for medium; and 150° for well-done beef. Remove from oven and let stand for 15 minutes. Internal temperature will increase 10°. This method of cooking beef does result in greater shrinkage, but the roast is very juicy, with a beautiful crusty exterior. Serve with roasted potatoes.

YORKSHIRE PUDDING

       2 cups (450 mL) flour
       ½ tsp (2 mL) salt
       3 eggs
       2 cups (450 mL) milk
       3 tbsp (45 mL) dripping from roast

Mix first four ingredients. Let stand 1 hour. Heat oven to 450°. Pour dripping into 9 x 9 in. (22 x 22 cm) baking pan and place in oven. When fat is hissing hot, pour in batter about 1 in. (2.5 cm) deep in pan. Bake 30 minutes or until puffed and golden.

CORNED BEEF

       3-4 lb (1.5-2 kg) beef brisket
       Brine:
        4 qt (5 L) water
        5 lb (2.5 kg) coarse salt
        2 cups (500 mL) brown sugar
        5 oz (150 g) saltpeter or potassium nitrate — optional
       15 peppercorns

Add salt to cold water; when a potato will float the brine is strong enough. Add rest of ingredients. The saltpeter is optional. It gives the meat a bright-red colour but it also toughens it slightly. Boil this brine for 25 minutes. Cool completely. Wipe the meat all over; cut off excess fat but there should be a good distribution of fat through the meat. Rub meat all over with additional salt, and saltpeter, if desired. Put in a large crock and pour cold brine over. Weight meat with an old plate to hold it under surface and leave in a cool place 4-6 days, turning meat once a day.

CORNED BEEF AND CABBAGE

       3-4 lb (1.5-2 kg) piece of corned beef
       1 small cabbage
       6 carrots, scraped
       1 small turnip, peeled
       6 medium potatoes, peeled
       dumpling batter

Wash the corned beef and place in large kettle with fresh cold water to cover. Bring slowly to the boil and simmer, without boiling, until meat is fork tender — about 2 hours. Skim the liquid to remove excess fat. Peel potatoes and leave whole. Cut cabbage in sixths. Cut turnip in 1 in. (2.5 cm) cubes. Leave carrots whole or cut in half lengthwise, if large, and crosswise if very long. Put carrots in with meat; cover and simmer; 15 minutes later add turnip and cabbage; 15 minutes later add potatoes; 5 minutes later put lumps of dumpling batter on the vegetables. Cover kettle and cook 20 minutes more. Remove vegetables and dumplings, slice meat and arrange on a platter. Broth may be served as a soup for first course.

CORNED BEEF HASH

2 cups (500 mL) cooked corned
  beef, cubed
3 medium cooked potatoes, diced
2 tbsp (30 mL) rendered beef fat
  skimming from boiled beef

¾ cup (185 mL) whipping cream
1 tsp (5 mL) steak sauce
1 tbsp (15 mL) finely chopped onion

Sauté the onion in frying pan in hot fat. In a bowl, combine beef, potatoes, cream, and steak sauce. Add the onions and mix carefully without mashing the potatoes. Heat the fat in the frying pan and fry the hash in thick cubes until the outsides are crisp and brown and the mixture heated through. The hash may be served with fried eggs. Note: butter can be used in place of beef fat.

PICKLED TONGUE

3 qt (4 L) water
1½ cups (375 mL) coarse salt
3½ oz (100 g) saltpeter — optional
½ cup (125 mL) white sugar

3 tbsp (45 mL) pickling spice in
  gauze bag
1 beef tongue, weighing 4 lb (2 kg)
salt

Combine the water and salt; brine should float a potato. Add saltpeter, sugar, and spices and bring to a boil. Cool and place in crock. Wash the tongue and trim off fat. Rub with more salt and immerse in brine solution with a plate to keep it down. Cover and keep in cool place for 8-10 days. Before cooking pickled tongue, soak overnight in fresh, cold water.

COLD BOILED TONGUE

1 beef tongue, fresh or pickled, weighing 3-4 lb (1.5-2 kg)
water
1 onion
3 cloves
1 carrot, scraped and sliced
1 stick of celery with leaves

If tongue is pickled, soak it overnight. If fresh, simply wash. Put in large kettle with water to cover. Add rest of ingredients. Bring to boil, skim, and simmer for 3 hours or till fork tender. Let cool in broth until the temperature is comfortable to handle. Cut off the root and peel off the skin. Fold tip of tongue over to root and push into a bowl just big enough to hold it. Cover with a plate and put a heavy weight on top. Chill overnight without removing weight. Turn out of bowl and slice.

BOILED HAM

1 ham — not precooked

Scrub the ham well with a brush. Cut off any hard tag ends. Place in a kettle with cold water to cover and boil ½ hour per lb (1 hour per kg). Let ham cool in the liquid. It is ready for baking.

BAKED HAM

1 boiled or precooked ham
1 cup (250 mL) brown sugar
⅓ cup (85 mL) orange juice, or, vinegar
1 tsp (5 mL) dry mustard
cloves
1 cup (250 mL) fine dry bread crumbs

Mix bread crumbs, brown sugar, and mustard. Peel off the skin of the ham and score the fat in diamond shapes. Place a clove at the points where the lines cross. Add enough juice to the sugar mixture to make a paste. Spread over the ham and bake in 300° oven for 15 minutes per lb (30 minutes per kg), basting from time to time with remaining juice or vinegar. If ham does not look brown enough, remove from oven, raise temperature to 500°, and replace ham for 5 minutes.

STUFFED HAM

2 slices ham ¼ in (0.5 cm) thick
2 tbsp (30 mL) flour
2 cups (500 mL) dry bread crumbs
¾ cup (180 mL) hot water
salt
½ tsp (2 mL) pepper
½ tsp (2 mL) savory
2 tbsp (30 mL) chopped apple
1 egg
½ cup (125 mL) milk
½ cup (125 mL) water

Moisten the bread with hot water and add next six ingredients. Flour one side of each slice of ham and spread half the stuffing on the other side of each slice. Roll up and tie with string. Place in baking dish with milk and water and bake 1 hour in 400° oven.

LEG OF LAMB

1 leg of lamb
2 cups (500 mL) bread dressing, more or less
salt and pepper
2 tbsp (30 mL) mint jelly, or, red currant jelly

Starting at the hip end — broader one — using a sharp, narrow-bladed boning knife, cut around the bones and push the meat back away from the bones. The first joint you come to will be the ball-and-socket, hip joint; when the meat is removed from this, follow along the shaft of the thigh bone until the knee joint is reached. Cut the tendons holding this joint together and remove the hip and thigh bones completely. Locate the small, triangular kneecap at the knee joint and cut it out, being careful not to cut right through the outside surface. Leave the end of the shank bone in place but cut away the meat surrounding it so that about an inch of clean bone protrudes from the end of the roast like a little handle. Rub the red part of the meat with a little savory and freshly ground pepper. Fill the space left by the bone with the dressing and close the open end by sewing with twine. Remove the papery skin — fell — covering the roast and also any excess fat which will be found on older beasts. Sprinkle well with salt and roast on a rack in 325° oven for 30 minutes per lb (1 hour per kg) —unboned weight. For the last 20 minutes of cooking time increase oven heat to 375° and brush the lamb all over with the jelly which has been melted. Let rest for 15 minutes before slicing. The protruding shank bone should be covered with foil while the roast is cooking, and may be dressed with a paper frill before serving. Remove string and slice vertically so each slice contains some stuffing. Serve with mint sauce.

MINT SAUCE

½ cup (125 mL) finely chopped mint leaves
½ cup (125 mL) water
½ cup (125 mL) cider vinegar
1-2 tbsp (15-30 mL) white sugar

Boil water, sugar, and vinegar together. Pour over mint leaves. Let cool to room temperature. Add more sugar if sweeter sauce is desired.

LAMB CHOPS

loin or rib chops
vinegar
freshly ground pepper
2 tsp (10 mL) sugar

Wipe chops with small amount of vinegar and cut off excess fat. Sprinkle with pepper. Heat a heavy cast-iron frying pan and sear chops on both sides. Lower heat and cook slowly until a sharp knife cut at the bone doesn't show pink. Deglaze the pan with ¼ cup (60 mL) boiling water with 1 tsp (5 mL) of vinegar and the sugar. Stir until all brown bits are removed from pan, and let boil 2 or 3 minutes until rich and brown. Season with salt and pour over chops.

STUFFED BREAST OF LAMB

4 lb (2 kg) breast of lamb
½ lb (250 g) ground lamb meat
2 cups (500 mL) bread dressing
1 egg, beaten
oil
salt and pepper

Mix Bread Dressing with ground lamb — if lamb is very lean add a little extra butter — and mix in beaten egg. Cut a pocket in the breast following the inner curve of the ribs. Fill loosely with stuffing and close with skewers. Brush meat all over with oil. Sprinkle with salt and pepper. Place in roasting pan, ribs down. Add ½ cup (125 mL) water. Cover and cook in 350° oven for 1½-2 hours or till tender. To serve, slice between ribs and serve two ribs per person.

BREAD DRESSING

2 cups (500 mL) soft bread crumbs
½ medium onion, chopped
1 tsp (5 mL) summer savory
1 tsp (5 mL) pepper
½ tsp (2 mL) salt
6 tbsp (100 mL) butter

Combine first five ingredients; rub butter in to make a mixture which just holds together when pressed into a ball.

LAMB SHANKS

6 lamb shanks
6 tbsp (90 mL) flour
2 tbsp (30 mL) shortening
1¼ cups (300 mL) water, or, red wine
2 tsp (10 mL) vinegar, or, mint sauce
salt and pepper

Use ¼ cup (60 mL) flour; roll the shanks in it until all are coated. Melt shortening in frying pan. Brown shanks and place in casserole. Add the rest of flour to fat and cook over medium heat 15 minutes until flour is well browned. Add water, vinegar, and salt and pepper to taste. Cook 3 or 4 minutes, stirring to loosen all the brown bits. Pour over shanks, cover and bake in 300° oven for 2 hours. Note: The substitution of red wine improves this dish greatly but if this is done the vinegar should be omitted.

ROAST PORK

6-8 lb (3-4 kg) fresh ham
salt and pepper
bread dressing
¼ cup (65 mL) apple jelly
apple juice

Bone the roast by the same method as for the leg of lamb. Fill the cavity with Bread Dressing. Score the heavy rind at 1 in. (2.5 cm) intervals cutting right through. Rub the whole roast with salt and pepper. Place on rack in shallow roaster in 325° oven and roast 35 minutes per lb (1¼ hours per kg), basting from time to time with apple juice. When roast is almost done, remove from oven and increase oven heat to 500°. Cut off the strips of rind leaving a very thin layer of fat. Thin the apple jelly with a little apple juice and spread over roast. Replace in oven for 10 minutes. Meanwhile lay strips of rind on rack in broiler pan. As soon as roast is glazed, place rind under heated broiler and broil, watching carefully until rind is puffed and crispy. Serve one piece of crackling with each serving. Make gravy with drippings.

OATMEAL PUDDINGS

5-6 large onions
¾ lb (350 g) beef suet
1 tbsp (15 mL) pepper
1 tbsp (15 mL) summer savory
1½ tbsp (25 mL scant) salt
6 cups (1.5 L) oatmeal
casings for 1 in. (2.5 cm) sausage

Chop the onions fine and chop the suet until it is the consistency of corn-meal. Combine with the rest of the ingredients and fill sausage casings. Pierce every 2 in. (5 cm) with a darning needle. Boil for 1 hour in a large pot of water. These puddings may be kept frozen. To serve, heat in a 350° oven for ½ hour. They may be heated in the roaster together with poultry or roast.

POT HAGGIS

½ lb (225 g) baby beef liver, or,
calves liver
1 sheep heart, or, veal heart, or,
2 lamb hearts
¼ lb (100 g) beef suet, finely ground

½ cup (125 mL) minced onion
1 cup (250 mL) rolled oats
dash of cayenne
1 tsp (5 mL) salt

Cover liver and heart with water. Bring to boil and simmer gently 1 hour. Reserve 1 cup (250 mL) stock. Cool meat; chill. Grind finely in food chopper. Render a little suet in a frying pan and lightly toast the oatmeal. Set aside. Gently sauté the onions until limp. Mix liver, heart, suet, onion, and oats together with stock. Add cayenne and salt. Put in a well greased bowl. Cover with 2 thicknesses of foil. Place on a rack in covered saucepan with water to come up halfway. Steam 2 hours. Turn out, slice, and serve.

POTTED HEAD

2 lb (1 kg) pork
3 lb (1.5 kg) beef shin — bone in
1 pig's foot
1 knuckle of veal
salt and pepper
2 tsp (15 mL) mixed pickling spice

Wash meat and bones. Remove marrow and fat. Put meat and bones in soup kettle; cover with cold water. Bring to a boil, skim, and simmer gently for 3 hours. Remove and drain the meat and chop it coarsely. Set aside, covered. Boil the bones for another hour to extract all the gelatin. Strain.

Tie the spices in a cheesecloth and continue cooking the liquid and spices until the liquid is reduced to half of original volume. Remove spice bag; return meat to kettle, and add salt and pepper to taste. Mix thoroughly and ladle mixture into bowls which have been rinsed in cold water. Chill until firm; serve, sliced, with salad.

BOILED STUFFED FOWL

1 fowl — do not use roasting chicken or broiler	½ lemon
1 onion	6 peppercorns
1 carrot	1 tsp (5 mL) salt per lb (0.5 kg) weight of bird
½ tsp (2 mL) celery seed	oatmeal stuffing

Clean the fowl well and rub with lemon juice. Stuff with ¾ cup (170 mL) Oatmeal Stuffing per lb (0.5 kg) weight of bird. Be sure not to overfill as stuffing swells. Sew opening closed, overlapping the skin to make a tight closure. Sew neck opening as well. Truss legs and wings close to the body and rub the bird with lemon. Wrap the bird in a cloth — a flour bag or old tea towel. This will keep it white and help it to hold its shape. Put the bird in a large stewing kettle with onion, carrot, peppercorns, salt, and celery seed. Cover with cold water. Bring to a boil and then simmer gently for 20 minutes per lb (45 minutes per kg). When the drumstick is soft when pinched, the bird is done.

If the fowl is to be eaten hot, it is removed from the stock, drained, unwrapped, sliced, and served. If it is to be served cold — the better method of serving this type of bird — it should be allowed to cool in the liquid; it should then be drained and dried well. It should be coated with aspic or sauce if it is to be kept whole; otherwise it can be sliced.

When the fowl has been removed, the stock should be strained and chilled. There will be about 8 cups (2 L). This reserved stock may be used as the base for delicious soup. See the recipes for Chicken Soup on page 97, and Cream of Chicken Soup on page 98.

OATMEAL STUFFING FOR BOILED FOWL

1 cup (250 mL) oatmeal — not rolled oats
¼ cup (60 mL) ground suet
2 tbsp (30 mL) finely chopped onion
1 tsp (5 mL) butter
pepper and salt

Sauté the onion in butter till limp. Mix with suet and oatmeal. Season with salt and pepper to taste.

ROAST TURKEY

1 turkey, weighing 8-16 lb (4-7 kg)
¾ cup (170 mL) bread stuffing per lb (0.5 kg) weight
¼ lb (100 g) butter

Rinse turkey cavity and pat dry. Sprinkle with salt. Using pliers, pull out white sinews from drumsticks. Using a larding pin, insert strips of butter under the skin of breast. If you do not have a larding pin small flat pats of butter can be worked under the skin with the fingers. Do this working from the neck cavity. Stuff breast and body cavity, without packing tightly. Skewer body opening closed and lace with string. Fold neck skin onto back and fasten with skewer. Fold wing tips onto back. Truss drumsticks together bringing ends of string across back and tie wings to body. Place turkey breast side down on an oiled rack and cover the bird with a cheesecloth soaked in melted butter. When three quarters of the cooking time has passed, remove the cheesecloth; turn turkey over; baste breast with pan dripping and continue roasting breast side up. Roast turkey in 300° oven 20-30 minutes per lb (0.5 kg) using the lower figure for heavier birds. Total time will be 3-5½ hours. The bird is done when drumstick moves easily. Let turkey rest 20 minutes before carving.

STUFFING FOR TURKEY

7 cups (1750 mL) bread crumbs
2 large onions, chopped
1 cup (250 mL) diced celery
¼ cup (65 mL) butter
1 tsp (5 mL) savory
1 tsp (5 mL) pepper

1 tsp (5 mL) salt
2 tbsp (30 mL) chopped parsley
¾ lb (350 g) sausage meat
1 cup (250 mL) oysters and juice
— optional

Combine all ingredients and pack loosely into cavity. Stuff turkey immediately before cooking and, afterwards, remove leftover dressing from cavity; store separately in a covered bowl.

PERFECT CRANBERRY SAUCE

4 cups (1 L) cranberries
1 cup (250 mL) water
2 cups (500 mL) sugar
½ tsp (2 mL) salt
¼ tsp (1 mL heaping) soda

Combine in a large saucepan and cook, very gently, covered for 15 minutes after you hear the first berry pop. Let stand for 24 hours and DO NOT REMOVE COVER. Every berry will be whole and crystal clear.

TURKEY CROQUETTES

2 tbsp (30 mL) butter
2 tbsp (30 mL) minced onion
6 tbsp (90 mL) flour
½ tsp (2 mL) salt
pinch of pepper
1½ cups (350 mL) milk

3 cups (725 mL) finely chopped
  cooked turkey
1 egg, beaten
2 tbsp (30 mL) water
fine dry bread crumbs

Melt butter. Add onion and sauté till brown. Blend in flour and add salt and pepper. Slowly add milk and stir until very thick. Mix in turkey and chill mixture until it will hold shape. With wet hands, on floured board, shape mixture into rolls 1 in. (2.5 cm) in diameter by 3 in. (7.5 cm) long. Mix egg and water. Dip croquettes into egg and then into bread crumbs and roll to cover. Chill 1 hour and then fry for about 5 minutes in deep fat heated to 375°F (190°C). Drain.

THANKSGIVING TUESDAY TURKEY PIE

5 strips of bacon
½ cup (125 mL) flour
4 cups (1 L) milk
1 tbsp (15 mL) chopped parsley
⅛ tsp (1 mL scant) dried savory
3 cups (750 mL) cooked turkey,
    large chunks

3 cups (750 mL) chopped leftover
    vegetables
1 recipe whole wheat biscuits
½ cup (125 mL) grated Cheddar
    cheese
salt and pepper

Fry bacon till crisp. Drain. Pour off fat and measure out ¼ cup (65 mL) and return this to pan. Add flour and cook slowly for 15 minutes. Gradually add milk, stirring till smooth. Cook, adding parsley, savory, salt, and pepper to taste. Cook until thickened; add turkey and vegetables, mixing well. Pour into large, ovenproof casserole. Make Whole Wheat Biscuits, adding cheese to recipe. Cut into 2 in. (5 cm) biscuits and arrange around edge of casserole. Crumble bacon and sprinkle over the centre. Bake 20 minutes in 425° oven. Serve with heated leftover dressing.

PUFFED TURKEY CASSEROLE

2 tbsp (30 mL) butter
3 tbsp (45 mL) flour
1 cup (225 mL) milk
1 tsp (5 mL) sugar
1 cup (225 mL) chopped cooked
    turkey

1 cup (225 mL) chopped celery
½ tsp (2 mL) salt
3 eggs, separated
½ cup (112 mL) leftover dressing,
    if any

Melt butter in saucepan. Stir in flour. Add milk, stirring. Cook until thick. Add egg yolks, off the heat, one at a time, beating after each one. Add turkey and celery. Beat egg whites with salt until stiff. Fold into turkey mixture. Pour half of mixture into a greased soufflé dish, or casserole, and sprinkle with leftover dressing, crumbled into crumbs. Cover with remainder of batter and bake 45-50 minutes in 375° oven.

TURKEY TURNOVERS

pastry for two-crust pie
2 cups (500 mL) sliced cooked turkey pieces, bite size
1 cup (250 mL) cooked diced potato
½ cup (125 mL) cooked leftover vegetables, diced
¾ cup (185 mL) turkey gravy

Combine turkey, vegetables, and gravy. Roll out pastry and cut into four rounds. Divide turkey mixture into four equal parts and place one part on half of each round. Moisten edges of pastry and fold round over. Pinch and seal. Bake 30 minutes in 425° oven.

ROAST DUCK

2 ducklings, weighing 4-5 lb (2-2.5 kg)
shells of 3-4 squeezed oranges — use juice for another purpose
6-7 hackmatack or juniper berries
½ cup (125 mL) orange marmalade, melted

Remove all loose fat from ducks. Wash and dry cavity of ducks and sprinkle with salt. Stuff with orange shells and juniper berries. It is not necessary to close opening, but tie drumsticks together. Cut off wing tips. Tie wings close to body. Sprinkle with salt and rub into skin. Prick all over with fork but be careful not to pierce through fat layer into meat. Place on rack in roaster and roast uncovered 1½ hours in 325° oven, or until drumstick moves easily. Remove from roaster and place rack in another pan or roaster lid. Increase oven heat to 500°. Brush birds all over with marmalade and glaze 10 minutes in oven. Do not do this last step in the roaster or the drippings will be spoiled for gravy. By changing pans, the gravy can be made while ducklings glaze. Serve ducks wearing necklaces of candied cranberries strung on threads. The ducks wear them that is!

ORANGE GRAVY

necks, giblets, and livers of 2 ducks
½ cup (125 mL) fresh orange juice
peel of 1 orange and 1 lemon
¾ cup (200 mL) heavy cream, scalded
 2 tbsp (30 mL) red currant jelly, melted
salt and pepper

Cover the necks and giblets of the duck with cold water and simmer, covered, for 2 hours. Add livers and simmer gently for a few minutes until just firm — about 15 minutes. Strain stock and set aside with liver. Peel the orange and lemon with a swivel peeler being sure not to cut into white pith. Shred the peel; cover with cold water; bring to a boil and drain. Pour off all the fat from the roasting pan in which ducks were roasted. Add orange juice and an equal amount of the stock from the giblets to the pan. Cook over medium heat, scraping bottom of pan to deglaze. Strain into small saucepan and boil hard until reduced to ½ cup (125 mL). Add the blanched peel and simmer 5 minutes. Blend in cream and melted jelly. Heat but do not allow to boil. Rub the livers through a sieve or food mill and add. Serve with duck.

CANDIED CRANBERRIES

1 cup (250 mL) fresh cranberries
1 cup (250 mL) sugar
1 cup (250 mL) water

Mix sugar and water in a wide heavy pan. Boil to 238°F (115°C). Prick each cranberry with a needle in 2 or 3 places. Add cranberries to syrup and cook gently till berries are clear. Remove berries to wax paper and let stand overnight. Roll berries in granulated sugar. Use to garnish or string on a thread to make necklace for roast duck or turkey.

BRAISED GOOSE

1 ready-to-cook goose over
   10 lb (4.5 kg)
salt
2 strips fat bacon
½ cup (125 mL) apple juice,
   or, cider
5 onions, quartered
3 carrots, sliced
goose giblets and neck

1 tbsp (15 mL) flour
salt
pepper
1 small whole onion
1 whole carrot
tart apple jelly

Wash the goose; cut off neck and wing tips. Dry bird inside and out. Sprinkle inside with salt and stuff with ½ cup (250 mL) potato dressing per lb (500 g). Close opening with skewers, lace, or sew with string. Rub outside with salt and lay strips of bacon over breast. The fat will be quickly drawn by the heat and will aid in drawing out the goose grease. Place goose on rack in large roast pan, which has a cover, and cook, *uncovered,* in 450° oven for 30 minutes. At the end of this time, pour off all accumulated fat; discard bacon; place quartered onions and sliced carrots in pan; add apple juice. Cover and replace in 325° oven.

Meanwhile, put neck, giblets and wing tips in water to cover with whole onion and carrot and simmer 1 hour or longer; strain. This may be done earlier in the day if convenient.

As soon as goose fat is poured off, take 1 tbsp (15 mL) of the grease and heat in a small saucepan. Add flour and blend. Cook until flour has browned and then blend in 2 cups (500 mL) of the stock made from neck and giblets. Simmer for 1 hour or until sauce is reduced to 1 cup (250 mL). At this time, pour into pan with goose together with 1 cup (250 mL) of stock. Add a little more apple juice if the pan looks dry.

Cook the goose for 4-4½ hours, or until tender. Transfer goose to platter and brush all over with melted apple jelly. Pour all liquid out of roasting pan and raise oven to 500°. Return goose to roasting pan and glaze 10 minutes in oven. Meanwhile skim fat off the pan sauce; season and serve.

POTATO DRESSING FOR GOOSE

6 cups (1.5 L) cooked potatoes,
   cut in ¾ in. (2 cm) cubes
3 large apples
1 egg
1 tsp (5 mL) savory
salt and pepper to taste

¼ tsp (1 mL) ground nutmeg
1 tbsp (15 mL) vinegar
¼ cup (50 mL heaped) chopped
   parsley

Boil potatoes until just barely tender; cube. Peel, core, and cut apples in eighths. Toss potatoes and apples together with vinegar. Season with salt, pepper, and savory, and sprinkle with ground nutmeg. Mix in the egg, lightly beaten, until each piece is coated. Lightly toss in parsley. Spoon into cavity of goose. Do not overfill. Clost cavity with skewers, or sew with string.

ROAST VENISON

5-6 lb (2.5-3 kg) roast of venison
1 onion, sliced
2 carrots, scraped and sliced
3 sprigs parsley
1 tsp (5 mL) salt

6 peppercorns
6 hackmatack or juniper berries
2 qt (2 L) red wine vinegar
1 cup (250 mL) oil
½ lb (250 g) fat salt pork

Combine onion, carrots, parsley, salt, peppercorns, and juniper berries with vinegar. Cut half of the salt pork into strips about ¼ x ¼ x 4 in. (0.5 x 0.5 x 10 cm). Pull the strips through the venison to lard it. Remove all the sinews and marinate the meat in the vinegar mixture. Add the oil to cover the surface and let stand 24 hours. Remove meat and wipe dry. Season with salt and cover with remainder of the salt pork. Roast 15 minutes per lb (35 minutes per kg) in 425° oven. Let stand 15 minutes before carving.

VENISON STEW

3-4 lb (1.5-2 kg) venison in
    1 in. (2.5 cm) cubes
salt and pepper
2 oz (55 g) salt pork, diced
1 turnip, peeled and sliced
4 onions, chopped

4 carrots, scraped, sliced
pinch of savory
2 tbsp (30 mL) flour
1 cup (250 mL) red wine, or,
    water

Season venison cubes in salt and pepper; roll in flour. Cook salt pork in heavy skillet until crisp and fat is rendered. Brown venison cubes all over. Add vegetables, wine, and savory. Reduce heat and simmer covered for 1½ hours or till meat is fork tender. Skim off excess fat. Serve with boiled potatoes and cooked mushrooms.

VENISON STEAK

2 lb (1 kg) venison steaks ¾ in. (2 cm) thick
1 tsp (5 mL) salt
2 tsp (10 mL) crushed peppercorns
walnut-sized piece of beef suet
2 tbsp (30 mL) boiling water, or, cognac

Season steaks with salt. Press pepper into steaks with side of a plate. Render fat in heavy skillet until very hot. Sear both sides of steaks; reduce heat a little and cook about 8 minutes. Venison should be rare. Remove venison to plate or board. Pour water or cognac in skillet, stir well to deglaze pan. Cook 1 minute; pour over steak.

WILD DUCK

2 wild ducks
salt and pepper
¼ cup (65 mL) butter
½ cup (125 mL) chicken broth, or, wine

Stuff birds with Tart Fruit Stuffing; season with salt and pepper. Roast covered in 325° oven for 1½ hours, basting with a mixture of butter and broth.

TART FRUIT STUFFING

2 apples, peeled, cored, and diced
2 oranges, sectioned, with
  membrane removed
1 cup (250 mL) soft bread crumbs
2 tbsp (30 mL) chopped parsley

4 tbsp (60 mL) melted butter
pinch of pepper
1 cup (250 mL) seedless
  green grapes

Toss together and use to stuff duck. Do not pack too full.

CASSEROLE OF PARTRIDGE

4 partridge, cleaned, with shot
  picked out
1 onion, chopped
½ cup (125 mL) butter
1½ cups (375 mL) beef stock —
  ½ cup (125 mL) dry sherry
  may be substituted for
  ½ cup stock
salt and pepper

½ tsp (2 mL) savory
3 apples, cored and peeled
1 cup (250 mL) water
1 cup (250 mL) whipping cream
½ cup (125 mL) sugar
2 tbsp (30 mL) rum
½ cup (125 mL) thick cranberry
  sauce

Melt butter in dutch oven. Brown the birds, breast side down; turn birds over, add onion, and brown birds on the other side. Remove birds; add broth and stir well to loosen all brown bits. Sprinkle birds with salt and pepper and powdered savory. Return birds to casserole and roast 30 minutes in 300° oven. Baste often. Make a syrup of sugar and water. Cut apples in eighths and poach in syrup till tender. Remove from syrup and mix with cranberries. Remove birds from casserole; keep warm. Over low heat, add cream to casserole and simmer 5 minutes. Check seasoning. Add rum. Garnish birds with fruit and serve sauce in gravy boat.

Puddings, Desserts, and Dessert Sauces

SPOTTY DOG OR SIX-CUP PUDDING

1 cup (250 mL) finely ground suet
1 cup (250 mL) fresh bread
  crumbs
1 cup (250 mL) flour
1 cup (250 mL) sugar —
  brown or white
1 tbsp (15 mL) baking soda

1 cup (250 mL) mixed fruit —
  raisins, currants, chopped
  dates, figs
1 cup (250 mL) milk, or, 1 egg
  plus enough milk to make
  1 cup (250 mL)

Mix flour and soda; then add other dry ingredients and fruit; and, finally, gradually stir in the milk. Grease a large pudding basin and fill three-quarters full. Cover with foil or cloth, tightly tied, and place on a rack in a steamer or kettle; add boiling water to come halfway up the sides of the basin. Cover kettle and steam 3 hours.

This pudding, or indeed any steamed pudding, may be cooked in the old-fashioned way, in a cloth which, while a little trickier, gives it a beautiful appearance. Here is the method: Make the pudding batter, using the egg alternative. Take a clean, closely-woven cotton cloth — a flour bag or a piece of sheeting about 24 in. (60 cm) square. Scald it in boiling water and wring it out. Spread it flat and dust the surface well with flour so that it is coated with dry flour granules. Carefully put the centre of the cloth over a mixing bowl and pour the pudding batter into the centre of the cloth. Gather up the edges of the cloth and tie it tightly, being sure you have left room for the pudding to swell. Try to arrange the folds of cloth so they do not "cut into" the batter too deeply. Lift the pudding by the "tail" and put it on an old plate in the bottom of the steamer. Cover with boiling water and boil for 3 hours. When cooked, lift the pudding out of the boiling water by the tail. Cut the string and carefully undo the cloth. There will be a "skin" on the pudding which you must not break. Gently roll the pudding over so the round, smooth side is uppermost. It will look like a "round, speckled cannonball' to quote Charles Dickens.

APPLE OATMEAL PUDDING ✕

4 apples	½ tsp (2 mL) vanilla extract
¼ cup (60 mL) white sugar	½ cup (120 mL) rolled oats
¼ tsp (1 mL) cinnamon	½ cup (120 mL) sifted flour
⅓ cup (80 mL) shortening	2 tsp (10 mL) baking powder
½ cup (120 mL) brown sugar	¼ tsp (1 mL) salt
1 egg	½ cup (120 mL) fresh milk

Peel, core, and cut apples in eighths. Arrange in a greased baking dish and sprinkle with cinnamon and white sugar mixed. Cream shortening; add brown sugar and cream. Add egg and beat well. Combine flour, rolled oats, baking powder, and salt. Add to creamed mixture alternately with milk. Fold in vanilla. Pour over apples and bake 40 minutes in 350° oven.

APPLESAUCE PUDDING

3 apples, peeled and cored	¼ tsp (1 mL) nutmeg
¾ cup (175 mL) molasses	¼ tsp (1 mL) allspice
⅓ cup (80 mL) butter	1½ tsp (7 mL) baking soda
2½ cups (600 mL) flour	½ cup (120 mL) water
¼ tsp (1 mL) salt	1 egg
1 tsp (5 mL) cinnamon	

Slice the apples and cook with molasses over low heat until they are tender. Stir in the butter and set mixture aside to cool. Sift the dry ingredients together; add the cooled apple mixture, water, and egg. Grease a 1½ qt (1.5 L) pudding basin. Cover with cloth or foil; tie, and steam on a rack in a kettle for 1½ hours. Let stand 5 minutes; uncover and unmold onto serving plate.

MAPLE PUDDING

1 cup (250 mL) hot maple syrup	2 tsp (10 mL) baking powder
1 tbsp (15 mL) shortening	pinch of salt
2 tbsp (30 mL) sugar	½ cup (125 mL) milk
1 medium (large) egg	chopped nuts
1 cup (240 mL) sifted flour	

Cream shortening and sugar. Add egg and beat. Sift flour with baking powder and salt; add, alternately with milk, to creamed mixture. Grease 1 qt (1 L) casserole. Pour in hot syrup. Spoon batter on top. Bake 25 minutes in 350° oven. Sprinkle with chopped nuts.

HONEYCOMB PUDDING

½ cup (125 mL) sugar
½ cup (125 mL) flour
½ cup (125 mL) molasses
¼ cup (65 mL) melted butter

¼ cup (65 mL) warm milk
½ tsp (2 mL) soda
2 eggs, well beaten

Mix all ingredients and stir well to be sure there are no lumps. Pour into a greased, ovenproof casserole, 1 qt (1L) size. Bake ½ hour in 350° oven.

PABLUM PUDDING

2 cups (500 mL) milk
2 cups (500 mL) "Mixed Cereal" Pablum
2 medium egg yolks

¼ cup (60 mL) sugar
rind and juice of 1 orange
2 medium egg whites
¼ cup (60 mL) sugar

Add Pablum to milk and bring to a boil. Add egg yolks, well beaten, and mixed with first amount of sugar. Grate orange rind and add, together with orange juice. Pour into a baking dish. Set in pan of water and bake in 350° oven for ½ hour. Make meringue by beating 2 egg whites with second lot of sugar and a pinch of salt. Put on top of pudding and continue to cook until golden. Serve with whipped cream.

SOUFFLE PUDDING

3 tbsp (45 mL) melted butter
6 tbsp (90 mL) flour
¾ cup (180 mL) milk
1 tsp (5 mL) vanilla extract

4 large eggs, separated
6 tbsp (90 mL) sugar
pinch of salt

Heat milk. Combine butter and flour in heavy saucepan. Pour in all the milk at once. Cook and stir constantly until the mixture cleans the pan. Put the mixture in a large mixing bowl and add the egg yolks, one at a time, beating well. Add the vanilla extract and all but 1 tbsp (15 mL) of the sugar. Beat the egg whites with the salt until stiff. Beat in the remaining sugar. Fold egg whites into yolk mixture. Butter a 1 qt (1 L) soufflé dish and sprinkle with sugar. Pour in batter. Place soufflé dish in a pan of water and bake 50 minutes in 350° oven. This soufflé can be unmolded if desired or, if left to cool, can be heated and repuffed later.

CARROT PUDDING

½ cup (125 mL) shortening
1 cup (250 mL) sugar
1½ cups (375 mL) grated raw
   carrot
1 cup (250 mL) grated raw
   potato
1 cup (250 mL) flour
1 tsp (5 mL) baking soda

1 tsp (5 mL) salt
¾ tsp (4 mL) mixed spices —
   cinnamon, nutmeg, cloves
½ cup (125 mL) raisins
½ cup (125 mL) currants
⅓ cup (75 mL) mixed peel
juice and grated rind of half
   a lemon

Cream shortening and sugar; add carrot and potato. Sift together dry ingredients. Add with raisins, currants, and peel. Stir in lemon juice and rind. Grease a pudding basin and fill three-quarters full. Cover with foil, or cloth, and tie tightly. Place in steamer or large kettle with water to come up halfway. Cover kettle and steam 2½-3 hours. Unmold and serve hot.

CHILDREN'S MILK-FLOUR PUDDING

2 tbsp (30 mL) sugar
3 tbsp (45 mL) flour
1 cup (225 mL) scalded milk
pinch of salt
½ tsp (2 mL) flavouring — vanilla,
   almond, caramel, etc.
food colouring — optional

Combine flour, sugar, and salt. Stir in milk gradually, whisking to avoid lumps. Cook over hot water till thick. Cover and cook 10 minutes. Stir in flavouring; add food colouring if desired. Pour into moistened jelly mold or custard cups. Chill until firm. This pudding is quick, simple, and more economical than packaged pudding mixes.

CHOCOLATE PUDDING

Melt ½ oz (15 g) of semisweet chocolate with the milk in the recipe for Children's Milk-Flour Pudding.

HOLIDAY RICE PUDDING

1½ cups (335 mL) long grained rice
2 cups (450 mL) milk
1½ tbsp (20 mL) grated orange rind
¼ tsp (1 mL) salt
6 egg yolks
2½ cups (565 mL) milk

¾ cup (170 mL) sugar
5 tsp (25 mL) vanilla extract
1½ packages gelatin
⅓ cup (75 mL) cold water
12 oz (335 g) mixed candied fruit
3 tbsp (40 mL) orange juice
1 pt (500 mL) whipping cream

Wash rice; drain; cover with 6 cups (1350 mL) boiling water. Bring to boil again; drain; return rice to saucepan. Add milk, orange rind, salt, and half the vanilla. Cover and simmer very gently for 30 minutes. Meanwhile beat egg yolks, milk, and sugar and cook over hot water till mixture coats a spoon. Add rest of vanilla and the gelatin softened in the cold water. Remove from heat and stir until gelatin dissolves. Add to rice mixture. Cool. Add fruit which has steeped several hours in the orange juice. Whip 1½ cups (335 mL) of the cream — add a little sugar if you like — and fold into cold rice and fruit mixture. Pour into a 1½ qt (2 L) mold, rinsed in cold water. Chill till firm. Unmold and garnish with rest of the cream, whipped.

JAM PUDDING

¼ lb (120 g) butter
¼ cup (60 mL) sugar
1¼ cups (300 mL) flour
2 eggs

2 tbsp (30 mL) milk
½ tsp (2 mL) baking powder
pinch of salt
¾ cup (10 mL) strawberry preserves, or, cherry preserves

Grease a 1½ qt (1.5 L) pudding basin. Pour in strawberry preserves; set aside. Cream butter and sugar. Add eggs and milk. Sift flour with baking powder and salt. Add to egg mixture, beating well. Batter will be very thick. Spread over preserves and cover basin with foil, tightly tied. Place on rack in a steamer and add boiling water to come halfway up. Cover and steam 1½ hours. To serve, remove foil and unmold pudding on serving plate. Preserves will run down outside, acting as sauce.

PLUM PUDDING

½ cup (125 mL) flour
1 tsp (2 mL) soda
1 tsp (2 mL) soda
½ tsp (1 mL) cinnamon
½ tsp (1 mL) nutmeg
1 cup (250 mL) soft bread crumbs
¼ cup (65 mL) brown sugar
½ lb (250 g) cut mixed peel
½ lb (250 g) seedless raisins
½ lb (250 g) currants
½ lb (250 g) chopped suet
3 apples peeled, cored, and diced
molasses

Have ready one 5-6 cup (1250-1500 mL), or two 3 cup (750 mL) pudding basins, or six small molds. Combine flour, soda, salt, spices in large mixing bowl. Stir well to blend. Stir in remaining ingredients, except molasses, and mix well. Add enough molasses to moisten mixture. Pack mixture into greased pudding basins filling to top. Cover with waxed paper and foil, or a cloth, and fasten with a string. Steam for 8 hours for large mold; 3 hours for medium; and 2 hours for individual molds. To serve, reheat by steaming for 1 hour. Unmold and serve with Hard Sauce. Rich suet and fruit puddings may be cooked in advance and stored. To store steamed puddings: After cooking, thoroughly cool pudding in original molds, covered. Allow to stand at room temperature for 24 hours to dry out. Then store in cool, dry place.

PUMPKIN PUDDING

2 cups (480 mL) flour
1½ tsp (7 mL) baking powder
¼ tsp (1 mL full) soda
1 tsp (5 mL) salt
1 tsp (5 mL) cinnamon
½ tsp (2 mL) allspice
¼ tsp (1 mL) ginger
¼ tsp (1 mL) nutmeg
½ cup (120 mL) butter
¼ cup (60 mL) sugar
¾ cup (180 mL) brown sugar, firmly packed
2 large (extra-large) eggs
¾ cup (180 mL) drained, cooked pumpkin
¼ cup (60 mL) molasses
1 cup (240 mL) chopped walnuts

Combine flour, baking powder, soda, salt, and spices. Cream butter and sugars until fluffy. Beat in eggs. Combine molasses and pumpkin, and add to creamed mixture, alternately, with dry ingredients. Stir in nuts. Fill a 1½ qt (1.5 L) greased pudding basin. Cover with foil and secure with string. Place on rack in steamer and add boiling water to come halfway up the side of pudding basin. Cover and steam 2½ hours. Turn out and serve hot with whipped cream, flavoured with the syrup from preserved ginger.

BLUEBERRY GRUNT

1 qt (1 L) blueberries
⅔ cup (175 mL) sugar
½ cup (125 mL) water
2 cups (500 mL) flour
4 tsp (20 mL) baking powder

½ tsp (2 mL) salt
1 tsp (5 mL) sugar
2 tbsp (30 mL) butter and lard
  mixed
½ cup (125 mL) milk, more or less

Combine berries, water, and sugar in a covered saucepan. Place on medium heat and bring to a boil. Simmer gently while making dumplings. Mix flour, baking powder, salt, and sugar. Rub in the fat — as for biscuits — and add enough milk to make a batter of dropping consistency. Drop by heaping tablespoons (25 mL measures), onto simmering berries. Cover and simmer 15 minutes, never raising the lid. Serve hot.

BAKED APPLES

1 Northern Spy apple per serving

Filling per Apple:
2 tbsp (30 mL) brown sugar
pinch of cinnamon
1 tsp (5 mL) butter

Core apples and cut a strip of peel off the top. Run the point of a knife around the middle of the apple but do not remove any skin. Fill the hole in each apple with the brown sugar and cinnamon mixed, and place the butter on top. Arrange in a baking dish; add ½ cup (125 mL) of hot water. Bake uncovered, basting occasionally, for 1 hour in 350° oven. Arrange apples in serving dish. Boil juice until thick; pour over apples.

AUNT JEAN'S APPLE DELIGHT

3-4 apples, peeled, cored
2 tbsp (30 mL) butter
¼ cup (65 mL) sugar
grated rind of 1 orange
2 tsp (10 mL) vanilla extract, or, rum

Grate the apples on the coarse side of a grater. Melt butter in a small skillet and sauté the apples in the butter, turning often until they are tender. Stir in sufficient sugar to sweeten to taste. Stir in orange rind and vanilla. Cool and serve with a dollop of whipped cream or Devonshire Clotted Cream. Apple Delight may be used in place of applesauce in many recipes.

APPLE FRITTERS

2 cups (500 mL) peeled, cored
apples, sliced crosswise,
¼ in. (0.5 cm) thick
1 cup (250 mL) flour
1½ tsp (8 mL) baking powder

¼ tsp (1 mL) salt
3 tbsp (45 mL) icing sugar
⅓ cup (85 mL) milk
1 large (extra-large) egg

Mix last six ingredients till smooth, and let batter stand for 1 hour. Dip apple rings in batter and fry in 375° (190°C) until delicate brown. Drain and sprinkle with confectioners' sugar.

APPLE DUMPLING

Suet Pastry:
2 cups (450 mL) all purpose flour
2 tsp (10 mL) baking powder
½ tsp (2 mL) salt
6 oz (170 g) finely chopped suet
5-7 tbsp (75-100 mL) ice water

Combine dry ingredients and cut in suet. Add enough ice water to form a soft pastry. Turn out on a board and knead very gently with finger tips for about half a minute. Flatten into a cake; chill 5 minutes and roll out ¼ in. (0.5 cm) thick.

Filling:
3 cups (750 mL) coarsely chopped, peeled apples
1 tbsp (15 mL) lemon juice
¼-½ cup (65-125 mL) sugar
pinch of ground nutmeg

Toss apples with lemon juice and add sugar to taste. Sprinkle with nutmeg. Line a greased 4 cup (1 L) pudding basin with three quarters of the pastry. Fill the bowl with apple mixture. Wet the edge of the pastry and cover the bowl with the remaining pastry. Pinch edges to seal. Cover with greased foil, secured with string. Place on rack in a steamer; add boiling water to come halfway up and steam 2½ hours. Serve with custard sauce. Gooseberries and cherries also make excellent fillings.

APPLE SLUMP

3 cups (750 mL) peeled, coarsely chopped apples
1 tbsp (15 mL) lemon juice
¼-½ cup (65-125 mL) sugar
½ tsp (2 mL) cinnamon
1 cup (240 mL) flour

2 tsp (10 mL) baking powder
¼ tsp (1 mL) salt
3 tbsp (45 mL) butter
½ tbsp (7 mL) sugar
⅓ cup (75 mL) milk

Combine dry ingredients; cut in butter until mixture resembles cornmeal. Stir in enough milk to make a soft biscuit dough. Fill a 4 cup (1 L) pudding basin with the apples, tossed with the lemon juice, cinnamon, and sugar. Roll out the biscuit dough, to the same diameter as the bowl, and cover the apple mixture with it. Cover with greased foil and tie with string. Place on rack in steamer and add boiling water to come halfway up the basin. Steam 1 hour. Remove from kettle; take off foil and invert on serving plate. Serve with cream or ice cream.

RUSSET APPLESAUCE

4 or 5 russet apples
½ cup (125 mL) water
¼ cup (65 mL) sugar
pinch of nutmeg — optional
1 tsp (5 mL) lemon juice
grated rind of half a lemon

Peel apples, quarter, and core. Cut into eighths and add water. Cover and cook gently 20 minutes. Add lemon juice, rind, and nutmeg. Add sugar, tasting as you do so, to determine exact amount. If you wait until the mixture has cooled slightly, you can judge the amount of sugar better and will use less. This sauce can be served chunky or pureed. Be sure the russet apples are well-flavoured; some lack flavour and taste like turnips — they will not make good sauce.

FLOATING ISLAND

    3 egg whites
    3 tbsp (45 mL) red currant jelly — not too stiff
1½ cups (300 mL) heavy cream
  ¼ cup (50 mL) sugar
  ½ tsp (2 mL) grated lemon rind
  ½ cup (100 mL) syrup from canned peaches,
    or, Madeira wine

Beat egg whites till soft peaks form. Gradually beat in jelly until stiff. Whip the cream and fold in sugar and lemon rind. Fold in syrup — Madeira wine is a good substitute. Pour into crystal bowl. Float islands of meringue on cream.

LEMON OR LIME SNOW

1 envelope unflavoured gelatin
¾ cup (175 mL) sugar
¼ cup (60 mL) cold water
1 cup (240 mL) boiling water

grated peel of 1 lemon, or, of 1 lime
¼ cup (60 mL) lemon juice, or,
  lime juice
2 egg whites

Sprinkle gelatin over cold water; let soften. Add sugar, peel, boiling water, and lemon juice. Stir until dissolved and let chill until mixture is the same consistency as the egg whites. Add the egg whites and whip until the mixture triples in volume and forms soft peaks. Pour into mold and chill quickly till firm — put in freezer for 20 minutes. Serve with thin custard sauce.

LEMON GELATIN

    1 envelope unflavoured gelatin
  ¼ cup (60 mL) lemon juice
  ¼ cup (60 mL) cold water
1½ cups (330 mL) very hot water
pinch of salt
    6 tbsp (75 mL) sugar, or, to taste

Sprinkle gelatin on cold water; let soften. Add hot water, sugar, salt, and lemon juice. Pour into jelly mold which has been dipped in cold water. Chill until firm.

Orange sections, with membrane removed, may be stirred in when the mixture has chilled to a syrupy consistency.

COFFEE GELATIN

1 envelope unflavoured gelatin	pinch of salt
¼ cup (50 mL) cold water	1 cinnamon stick
1¾ cups (350 mL) hot coffee	cream
6 tbsp (75 mL) sugar, or, to taste	

Sprinkle gelatin on cold water; let soften. Add coffee, sugar, and salt. Stir with cinnamon stick and leave stick in until cool. Pour into cups and chill till firm. Serve with cream.

BAVARIAN CREAM

1 envelope, or 1 tbsp (15 mL) unflavoured gelatin	¼ tsp (1 mL) salt
¼ cup (50 mL) cold water	1 cup milk (200 mL)
2 large (small) egg yolks	1 tsp (5 mL) vanilla extract
½ cup (100 mL) sugar	2 large (small) egg whites
	1 cup (200 mL) whipping cream

Soften gelatin in water. Beat egg yolks slowly, adding half the sugar and the salt. Very gradually stir in milk. Place in top half of double boiler and cook over very hot — not boiling — water until slightly thickened. Add the softened gelatin, stirring till dissolved. Add vanilla extract. Strain and cool but do not allow to set. When mixture is slightly jelled, beat the egg whites until stiff but not dry, beating in remaining sugar. Fold into gelatin mixture. Whip cream stiff. Fold into mixture. Cut candied fruit or toasted almonds may be folded in at this point if desired. Rinse a jelly mold with cold water, pour in cream, chill until firm. Turn out by dipping mold in hot water and inverting on a plate. Note: Metric measurements give slightly smaller amount.

CHERRY CREAM

1 cup (200 mL) whipping cream
⅓ cup (65 mL) cherry preserves
2 cups (400 mL) chocolate cookies, crushed
with a rolling pin
½ dark chocolate bar, grated

Whip cream stiff. Set a bit aside and combine the rest with the coarse cookie crumbs. Layer in sherbet or parfait glasses with the cherry preserves. Top with plain cream and sprinkle with grated chocolate.

MAPLE CUSTARD

2 cups (500 mL) scalded milk
¼ tsp (1 mL) salt
4 tbsp (65 mL) grated maple sugar
4 medium (extra-large) egg yolks
¾ tsp maple flavouring — optional
1 cup (250 mL) maple syrup

Boil maple syrup till very thick. Divide among six custard cups. Beat the egg yolks; add sugar and salt. Stir in scalded milk and mix until all sugar is dissolved. Strain and pour into cups. Place dishes in a pan of hot water and cook in 325° oven until a silver knife inserted into the centre comes out clean. Cool and chill. Run a knife point around edge; invert over serving plate and shake out gently. The syrup will be runnier than that of crème caramel.

MAPLE PARFAIT

1½ cups (300 mL) maple syrup
3 (small) eggs
1 tsp (6 mL) gelatin
¼ cup (65 mL) cold water
2½ cups (500 mL) whipping cream

In a double boiler over very hot water, heat the syrup. Beat the eggs and stir into the hot syrup. Cook over hot water, stirring, till mixture thickens. Soften the gelatin in cold water; add to hot egg mixture and cool. Fold in 1 pt (500 mL) of whipping cream, whipped stiff. Freeze and serve with pecans and maple syrup.

HOMEMADE ICE CREAM

1½ cups (375 mL) whole milk — not 2%
3 large (extra-large) eggs
¾ cup (180 mL) sugar
½ tsp (2 mL) salt
1 tbsp (15 mL) vanilla extract
3 cups (750 mL) light, 10% cream
1 tbsp (15 mL) flour

Scald milk. Beat eggs; add sugar, flour, and salt, and gradually add milk, beating all the while. Put in top half of double boiler and cook over hot water till mixture coats a spoon. Cool. Add cream and vanilla; chill. Place in freezer can. Insert dasher cover; place in ice bucket and adjust crank. Use 1 part coarse salt to 8 parts crushed ice. Using too much salt will make ice cream grainy. Turn crank until the ice cream is frozen. Remove can. Take out dasher and recover can. Replace in ice bucket covering completely with 1 part salt to 4 parts ice, packing firmly around can. Let stand 3 or 4 hours. Chocolate chips, sweetened, crushed strawberries, or sliced peaches may be added before freezing.

BUTTERSCOTCH ICE CREAM

4 tbsp (60 mL) butter
1½ cups (360 mL) brown sugar
1 cup (240 mL) boiling water
8 (9) egg yolks

4 tbsp (20 mL) vanilla extract
4 cups (1 L) whipping cream
pinch of salt

Melt the butter; add sugar and stir till the sugar is melted. Boil gently for 1 minute; add boiling water and continue cooking and stirring until sugar mixture is dissolved. Beat egg yolks till thick and pour syrup into them, beating all the while. Cool and chill; whip cream and fold into egg yolk mixture. Add vanilla and salt. This mixture may be frozen in the freezer part of the refrigerator but has a better texture if frozen in an ice cream freezer, either electric or hand-cranked.

CLARA'S CURDS OR COTTAGE CHEESE

1 gal (5 L) skim milk
3 tbsp (50 mL) sour skim milk, or,
    4 junket tablets dissolved in 1 tbsp
    (15 mL) water
salt
cream — optional

Bring skim milk to 70° temperature. Add sour milk. Stir and leave over-night to set. Stir to break up the curds and heat the mixture over hot water. The water should be heated to 150°F (65°C) and the curds held at a temperature of 110°F (43°C) for sufficient time to secure a good separation of curds and whey. If the curds are overheated they will be dry and grainy. When a bit of curd does not appear milky when pinched between thumb and forefinger, the whey can be strained off through several thicknesses of cheesecloth. When the whey is strained off, the curds can be washed with cold water which removes the acid flavour. After washing, drain the curds well and then add salt to taste. When this is done, 1-2 tbsp (15-30 mL) of cream can be added, if desired.

DEVONSHIRE CLOTTED CREAM

1 qt (1 L) heavy unpasteurized cream

Place cream in a large, heavy pan set on a rack in a large roasting pan. Pour water into the roasting pan until it comes up the side of the pan of cream. Cook, barely simmering for 4 hours. Let cool and chill. There will be a firm heavy crust or clot of cream on the top. Lift off carefully. Discard the whey which is left underneath. Chill, and serve with fruit pies, fresh berries, or shortcake. Note: This may be made in a bowl, set in a large crock pot with 2 cups (500 mL) of water and cooked for 5-6 hours on low setting.

LEMON SAUCE

1 tbsp (15 mL) cornstarch	2 tbsp (30 mL) butter
½ cup (120 mL) sugar	pinch of salt
1 cup (240 mL) water	grated rind of 1 lemon
2 tbsp (30 mL) lemon juice	

Mix sugar and cornstarch and gradually add water. Bring to a boil over medium heat and cook until mixture is clear. Take off heat and stir in lemon juice, salt, butter, and grated lemon rind. If sauce is too thick, it may be thinned with a little more water or lemon juice.

CHERRY SAUCE

4 lb (2 kg) sour cherries
4 lb (2 kg) sugar

Stem and pit cherries. Combine cherries and sugar and cook slowly in a heavy pan for 1-1½ hours, till mixture is thick and syrupy. Do not add any water. Stir frequently. Ladle into sterilized jars and store. Use as a sauce with ice cream.

CHOCOLATE SAUCE

¾ cup (175 mL) brown sugar
¾ cup (175 mL) white sugar
pinch of salt
¾ cup (175 mL) grated
   unsweetened chocolate

1 cup (240 mL) whole milk, or,
   half whole milk and half
   light cream
1½ tbsp (20 mL) butter
1 tsp (5 mL) vanilla extract

Combine sugars, salt, chocolate, and milk in saucepan and cook, stirring, till sugar is dissolved and chocolate melted. Then, cook slowly without stirring until syrup reaches 224°F (106°C). Remove from heat; add butter and vanilla. Serve warm.

CUSTARD SAUCE

3 tbsp (50 mL) flour
½ cup (125 mL) sugar
pinch of salt
2 medium (large) eggs
2 cups (500 mL) milk
1 tsp (5 mL) vanilla extract

Mix flour, sugar, and salt in the top of double boiler. Add beaten eggs and then gradually add the milk which has been scalded. Cook over hot water, stirring continually, until mixture thickens. Add vanilla extract. Cool.

FOAMY SAUCE

1 egg, separated
½ cup (125 mL) sugar
½ cup (125 mL) whipping cream
1 tsp (5 mL) vanilla extract

Beat the egg white till foamy and gradually add half the sugar, beating till the whites are stiff and glossy. Whip the cream with the remaining sugar. Beat the egg yolk and fold into the cream, together with vanilla. Fold in egg whites.

HARD SAUCE

¼ cup (65 mL) butter
½ cup (125 mL) brown sugar
¼ cup (65 mL) dark rum, or, brandy

Cream the butter and sugar until well-blended and fluffy. Beat in the rum until blended. Chill till firm. Hard sauce may be made with icing sugar, but it is not as rich in flavour.

Pastry, Pies, Cookies, and Squares

PIE PASTRY

2 cups (480 mL) pastry flour
½ tsp (2 mL) salt
⅔ cup (160 mL) shortening, or, lard, or,
   half butter and half shortening
5-6 tbsp (75-90 mL) ice water

Sift flour with salt into bowl. For flaky pastry use a pastry blender or two knives, and cut the fat into the flour till it is like cornmeal, with some pieces of fat the size of peas. Sprinkle water over surface and mix with a fork as lightly as possible. Draw paste into a ball and chill. Roll out and use according to pie recipe. Makes sufficient for a two-crust pie.

PEACH PIE

4 cups (1 L) peaches, peeled,
   sliced
¾-1 cup (175-250 mL) sugar
3 tbsp (50 mL) quick-cooking
   tapioca

¼ tsp (1 mL) salt
1 tbsp (15 mL) lemon juice
1 tbsp (15 mL) butter
pastry for two-crust pie

Combine sugar, tapioca, and salt. Peel and slice peaches; add lemon juice and toss with sugar mixture. Let stand for 15 minutes. Roll out pastry and line 9 in. (22 cm) pie plate. Stir fruit mixture and fill shell. Dot with butter. Moisten edges of bottom crust and weave a lattice top. Fold excess bottom crust over the ends of the strips and crimp. Bake 50-60 minutes in 400° oven. Serve with whipped cream.

APPLE PIE

pastry for two-crust pie
4 or 5 apples
sugar
¼ tsp (1 mL) fresh, ground
   nutmeg

1 tbsp (15 mL) butter
1 tbsp (15 mL) vanilla extract,
   or, rum
1 tbsp (15 mL) lemon juice

Peel and core apples. Cut in thick slices or in chunks whichever you prefer. Place the peelings and the cores in a small saucepan with about ½ cup (125 mL) water and 1½ tbsp (20 mL) sugar. Put on stove; bring to boil; cover and simmer while pie is baking. Sprinkle apples with lemon juice and add sugar, tossing until the slices have a thin coat of sugar. Taste a piece of apple and, if it is still tart, add a little more sugar until a piece of apple tastes just right. Pile into a pastry-lined 8 or 9 in. (20 or 22 cm) pie plate; dot with butter; sprinkle with vanilla and nutmeg, and cover with a top crust which has a 1 in. (2.5 cm) hole cut in the centre instead of slits. Bake 50 minutes in 400° oven. When cooked, set pie to cool on rack. Remove the peelings and cores from the saucepan and, over a high heat, reduce the liquid to 2 tbsp (30 mL). Pour through hole in the pie and tip this way and that to distribute evenly.

LATE-IN-THE-SEASON APPLE PIE

pastry for two-crust pie
juice of 1 lemon
grated rind of 1 lemon
   3 cups (750 mL) peeled, sliced
      apples
¼ cup (65 mL) orange marmalade

¼ cup (65 mL) chopped, mixed peel
⅓ cup (85 mL) seedless raisins
¼ cup (65 mL) fine, dry bread
   crumbs
¼ cup (65 mL) sugar
2 tbsp (30 mL) butter

Warm the marmalade till it gets runny; mix it with all the other ingredients and put in pastry-lined 9 in. (22 cm) pie plate. Dot with butter and cover with pastry. Crimp and seal. Bake in 425° oven for 15 minutes; then in 350° oven for 30 minutes more.

BLACKBERRY AND APPLE PIE

pastry for a two-crust pie
3 early August apples
1 qt (1 L) blackberries
¼-½ cup (60-120 mL) sugar
1 tbsp (15 mL) butter

Pick over the blackberries, discarding any very small, seedy ones or any that are mushy. Peel, core, and slice apples very thin. Toss apples, blackberries, and sugar to taste in a large bowl. If apples are slightly underripe more sugar will be needed. Line 9 in. (22 cm) pie plate with pastry; fill with apple-berry mixture; dot with butter and cover with pastry. Crimp and seal. Bake in 425° oven for 35 minutes. Let cool but do not chill. Serve with Devonshire Clotted Cream or whipped cream.

BLUEBERRY PIE

pastry for two-crust pie
1 qt (1 L) fresh blueberries
1 cup (225 mL) sugar
1 tsp (5 mL) vinegar

2 tbsp (30 mL) flour
2 tbsp (30 mL) butter
white of egg, lightly beaten

Line 9 in. (22 cm) pie plate with pastry. Brush the shell lightly with egg white and set in 450° oven for 2 minutes. Remove from oven and fill with blueberries, tossed in a mixture of sugar and flour. Sprinkle with vinegar; dot with butter; cover with upper crust. Crimp and seal. Reduce oven to 425° and bake 25 minutes more. Cool on rack and serve with ice cream or sour cream .The egg white brushed on the bottom shell seals it and prevents the purple juice from soaking into the lower crust.

RASPBERRY PIE

pastry for a two-crust pie
2½ cups (625 mL) raspberries
½ cup (125 mL) brown sugar
1 tsp (5 mL) cornstarch
1 tbsp (15 mL) butter
white of egg

Line 9 in. (22 cm) pie plate with pastry and brush with egg white. Add the berries; sprinkle with sugar and cornstarch mixed. Dot with butter. Cover with upper crust. Bake for 10 minutes at 450°F; then reduce oven to 400° and bake 30 minutes longer.

CHERRY PIE

pastry for two-crust pie
2½ cups (625 mL) pitted sour cherries
¾ cup (180 mL) sugar — more if cherries
are very sour
3 tbsp (45 mL) flour
1 tbsp (15 mL) butter
pinch of salt

Line 9 in. (22 cm) pie plate with pastry. Mix sugar, flour, and salt and toss with cherries, mixing well. Pour into pie plate and dot with butter. Weave strips of pastry into a lattice top. Bake in 400° oven for 40 minutes.

MAMA MURRAY'S RAISIN CRANBERRY PIE

pastry for two-crust pie
1 cup (250 mL) cranberries, coarsely chopped
¾ cup (185 mL) seedless raisins
⅔ cup (170 mL) sugar

1 tbsp (15 mL) flour
¼ tsp (1 mL) vanilla
1 tbsp (15 mL) butter

Line 9 in. (22 cm) pie plate with pastry. Mix sugar and flour and toss with cranberries and raisins. Place in lined pie plate; dot with butter and sprinkle with vanilla. Cover with top crust. Crimp and seal. Bake 30 minutes in 425° oven.

RHUBARB PIE

pastry for two-crust pie
3 cups (750 mL) rhubarb in
1 in. (2.5 cm) pieces
1½ cups (375 mL) sugar
1 tbsp (15 mL) grated orange
rind
1 tbsp (15 mL) flour

1½ tbsp (25 mL) instant tapioca
½ tsp (2 mL) salt
1 tbsp (15 mL) lemon juice
1 tbsp (15 mL) butter
1 egg white
small amount sugar

Combine sugar, flour, tapioca, orange rind, and salt. Sprinkle the rhubarb with lemon juice and toss in the sugar mixture till all the rhubarb is coated. Pile in pastry-lined 9 in. (22 cm) pie plate. Dot with butter and cover with a lattice-top pastry. Brush the top of the pastry with lightly beaten egg white and sprinkle with sugar. Cook 40-50 minutes in 400° oven.

SQUASH PIE

pastry for one-crust pie
1 cup (250 mL) sugar
⅛ tsp (1 mL very scant) cinnamon
⅛ tsp (1 mL very scant) nutmeg
pinch of salt
1 tbsp (15 mL) melted butter

½ tsp (2 mL) ginger
2 cups (500 mL) hot milk
2 cups (500 mL) strained, cooked
squash'
3 beaten eggs

Roll out pastry and line an 8 or 9 in. (20 or 22 cm) pie plate. Mix sugar, salt, and spices. Blend in milk, squash, eggs, and butter. Pour into unbaked pie shell and bake 40 minutes in 425° oven, or until a knife blade, inserted, comes out clean. If there is too much filling, surplus may be baked in custard cups set in pan of hot water. Do not bake together with the pie because the steam from the water will make the pie soggy.

GRANDMA BOND'S MINCEMEAT PIE

5 cups (1250 mL) chopped
cooked beef, or, venison
2 cups (500 mL) chopped suet
7½ cups (1875 mL) chopped,
peeled apples
3 cups (750 mL) cider
½ cup (125 mL) cider vinegar
1 cup (250 mL) molasses
5 cups (1250 mL) white sugar
2½ cups (625 mL) seeded raisins,
cut up
1½ cups (375 mL) seedless raisins

juice of 2 lemons and 2 oranges
2 tsp (10 mL) cinnamon
2 tsp (10 mL) cloves
2 tsp (10 mL) allspice
2 tsp (10 mL) nutmeg
1½ cups (375 mL) brandy, or, rum
1 cup (250 mL) cherry preserves,
or, tart jelly
rind of lemon and oranges, shaved
off and cut fine
pastry for two-crust pie

Combine all ingredients in large kettle. Take the peels of the apples and simmer with 1 cup (250 mL) water and ¼ cup (65 mL) of sugar. Simmer 30 minutes. Strain into rest of ingredients and simmer for 1½ hours. Moisten with meat stock if mincemeat gets too thick. To make pie, roll out pastry and line a 9 in. (22 cm) pie plate. Fill with mincemeat. Cover with top crust. Cut a small hole in the middle. Bake in 425° oven for 45 minutes. Serve piping hot with 1 tbsp (15 mL) of dark rum or brandy poured through the hole in the top crust.

LEMON PIE

1 baked pie shell
1 cup (250 mL) sugar
¼ cup (65 mL) flour
pinch of salt
1 cup (250 mL) water

3 medium (large) eggs,
  separated
2 tbsp (30 mL) butter
¼ cup (65 mL) lemon juice
grated rind of 1 lemon

Mix sugar, flour, and salt. Add water a little at a time, stirring so no lumps form. Beat egg yolks and add. Cook over hot water, stirring constantly, till mixture thickens. Cover and cook 10 minutes more. Remove from heat; add butter, stirring to blend; stir in lemon juice and rind. Pour into baked 8 or 9 in. (20 or 22 cm) pie shell. Cover with meringue and bake in 350° oven for 10 minutes.

MOTHER'S NEVER-EVER-FAIL MERINGUE

1 tbsp (15 mL) cornstarch
2 tbsp (30 mL) cold water
½ cup (125 mL) boiling water
1 tsp (5 mL) vanilla extract

3 egg whites
6 tbsp (90 mL) sugar
pinch of salt

Blend cornstarch and cold water in saucepan. Add boiling water and cook until thick and clear. Cool completely. Beat egg whites till foamy; gradually beat in sugar, beating until stiff and glossy. Add salt and vanilla and slowly beat in cold cornstarch mixture. Beat quickly for several minutes. Spread meringue on filled, cooled pie shell. Bake 10 minutes in 350° oven.

LIMEY COCONUT CREAM PIE

8 in. (22 cm) baked pie shell
⅓ cup (80 mL) cornstarch
½ tsp (2 mL) salt
¼ cup (60 mL) cold water
1¼ (300 mL) hot water
3 medium (large) egg yolks
grated rind of 1 lime —
  if available
½ cup (120 mL) flaked coconut

⅓ cup (80 mL) lime juice —
  fresh or bottled
3 tbsp (45 mL) butter
toasted flaked coconut
1 cup (240 mL) whipping cream
1 tbsp (15 mL) confectioners'
  sugar
1 cup (240 mL) sugar

In top of double boiler mix half of sugar, cornstarch, cold water, and salt. Stir until smooth. Add hot water and cook, stirring, till thick. Beat egg yolks with other half of sugar and add small amount of hot mixture to egg yolks and then pour the whole egg yolk mixture back into double boiler. Cook, stirring, 3 minutes more. Remove from heat and stir in lime juice, rind, butter and ½ cup (120 mL) coconut. Pour into pie shell and cool. Whip cream with sugar and pile on filling, sprinkling with toasted coconut.

CUSTARD PIE

pastry for one-crust pie
3 medium (large) eggs
¼ cup (65 mL) sugar
¼ tsp (1 mL) salt

2¼ cups (565 mL) milk
2 tsp (10 mL) vanilla extract
nutmeg

Roll out pastry and line an 8 or 9 in. (20 or 22 cm) pie plate. Beat eggs lightly; add sugar, salt, milk, and vanilla. Pour into pie shell; sprinkle with nutmeg. Bake in 425° oven for 40 minutes, or until knife inserted in centre comes out clean.

BRAZIL NUT COOKIES

½ cup (125 mL) butter
1 cup (250 mL) brown sugar
1 large (extra-large) egg
1½ tsp (7 mL) vanilla extract
2 cups (500 mL) flour
¾ tsp (4 mL) soda
¾ tsp (4 mL) baking powder

¼ tsp (1 mL) salt
½ tsp (2 mL) nutmeg
½ tsp (2 mL) cinnamon
⅓ cup (85 mL) sour cream
½ cup (125 mL) chopped Brazil nuts
2 or 3 Brazil nuts

Cream butter and sugar. Add egg and vanilla. Sift the dry ingredients together and add, alternating with sour cream, to the creamed mixture. Add chopped nuts. Drop by teaspoonfuls on greased cookie sheet. Bake 10 minutes in 400° oven. Cool and frost with Butterscotch Icing. Garnish with shavings of the 2 or 3 Brazil nuts.
To shell Brazil nuts cover them with cold water; bring to the boil; boil 5 minutes; drain and plunge into cold water. Let stand 1 minute and drain. Crack shells with nutcracker and nuts will slip out whole.

BUTTERSCOTCH ICING

3 tbsp (45 mL) butter
2 cups (500 mL) icing sugar
2 tbsp (30 mL) milk
1 tsp (5 mL) vanilla extract

Heat butter and cook till brown. Stir in icing sugar, milk, and vanilla. Spread on Brazil Nut Cookies.

BROWN SUGAR SHORTBREAD

1 cup (250 mL) butter
½ cup (125 mL) brown sugar, packed
2½ cups (625 mL) flour

Cream butter and sugar until fluffy. Work in flour with the hand. Refrigerate until firm enough to handle. Roll out on lightly floured board ⅓ in. (0.8 cm) thick. Cut with cookie cutter. Place on cookie sheets, lined with brown paper. Bake 25 minutes in 300° oven.

SCOTS SHORTBREAD

2 oz (100 g) fruit sugar
4 oz (200 g) butter
6 oz (300 g) flour

Always weigh ingredients for best results and use the proportions of 1:2:3. Place all ingredients together on table and work with the hand until uniform and dough will hold together. Pat out — do not roll — ½ in. (1 cm) thick; cut with cutters or use wooden shortbread molds if you have them. Place on cookie sheets lined with brown paper and prick tops with fine side of nutmeg grater. Bake in 300° oven for 25 minutes. Do not allow to brown.

HOLIDAY WHIPPITS

½ cup (110 mL) butter
1 cup (225 mL) flour
2 tbsp (25 mL) brown sugar
pinch of salt
½ tsp (2 mL) baking powder
1½ envelopes gelatin
1 cup (225 mL) icing sugar
1 cup (225 mL) granulated sugar

1 cup (225 mL) cold water
pinch of salt
½ tsp (2 mL) vanilla extract
½ tsp (2 mL) baking powder
¼ cup (65 mL) red jelly — raspberry, red currant, or, strawberry
1 slice candied pineapple, cut up
4 squares semisweet chocolate

Combine butter, flour, brown sugar, salt, and baking powder, in that order. Pat into an 8 x 8 in. (20 x 20 cm) ungreased pan and bake in 350° oven for 10 minutes or till firm when touched. Cool and spread with warmed red jelly. Set aside. Soften gelatin in cold water in saucepan. Add granulated sugar and boil slowly for 10 minutes. Remove from heat; add icing sugar and let cool. Add vanilla and baking powder and whip until thick. Add pineapple. Pour over the baked mixture in pan. Refrigerate. When cold, melt chocolate and pour over. Mark in squares before chocolate has hardened completely. Store in refrigerator.

AUNT JEAN'S CHRISTMAS CHERRIES

½ cup (125 mL) butter
¼ cup (65 mL) sugar
1 large (extra-large) egg, separated
½ tsp (2 mL) vanilla extract
1 tbsp (15 mL) grated orange rind

1½ tsp (7 mL) grated lemon rind
1 tbsp (15 mL) lemon juice
1 cup (250 mL) cake flour
½ cup (125 mL) ground walnuts
halved candied cherries, red and green

Cream the butter and sugar until fluffy; add egg yolk, vanilla, orange and lemon rind, and lemon juice. Mix well and add flour. Chill well, for the dough is sticky. Roll the dough into little balls, dip in lightly beaten egg white and roll in walnuts. Put half a cherry on top of each. Place on lightly greased cookie sheet. Bake 20 minutes in 350° oven.

CHRISTMAS COOKIES

½ cup (125 mL) honey
¼ tsp (1 mL) salt
2 oz (60 g) candied cherries, chopped
1 medium (large) egg white
1 cup (250 mL) rolled oats
2 oz (60 g) chopped mixed peel

Spread rolled oats on a cookie sheet and toast in 350° oven, stirring often until pale brown. Let cool. Beat egg white with salt. Add liquid honey gradually. Fold in rolled oats and fruit. Drop by spoonfuls on greased cookie sheet. Bake 10 minutes in 350° oven.

GINGERSNAPS

¾ cup (225 mL) butter and lard
   mixed, approximately half
   and half
1½ cups (450 mL) white sugar
2 large (3 small) eggs
1 tsp (6 mL) cinnamon

1 tsp (6 mL) ginger
¾ tsp (5 mL) cloves
4 tsp (25 mL) soda dissolved in
   4 tsp (25 mL) water
4 cups (1200 mL) pastry flour
¾ cup (225 mL) molasses

Cream fats and sugar — it is important to include a portion of lard for snappy gingersnaps. Add eggs and molasses. Sift flour with spices and mix into batter. Last of all, mix in water and soda. Mix well, and chill for at least 2 hours before rolling ¼ in. (0.5 cm) thick. If dough sticks to rolling pin, roll between sheets of wax paper. Cut with large scalloped cutter, floured between cuts, and place on greased cookie sheets. Bake 12-15 minutes in 375° oven.

BRANDY SNAPS

½ cup (120 mL) molasses
½ cup (120 mL) butter
1¼ cups (300 mL) sifted cake
   flour

pinch of salt
⅔ cup (160 mL) sugar
1 tbsp (15 mL) ground ginger
3 tbsp (45 mL) brandy

Heat molasses to boiling. Add butter and melt. Remove from heat. Add sifted flour, salt, sugar, and ginger. Add brandy and stir. Batter should hold its shape, so hold back some of the brandy if necessary. Have several greased cookie sheets ready but make only six cookies at a time. Drop ½ tsp (2 mL) of batter 3 inches apart and bake in 300° oven for 10 minutes. Cool 1 minute; remove with metal spatula and roll around handle of a wooden spoon to form a hollow cylinder. This is the traditional brandy snap shape. If desired, brandy snaps can be piped full of whipped cream.

MAPLE COOKIES

1 cup (240 mL) shortening
⅔ cup (160 mL) grated maple sugar
1 medium (large) egg
3 cups (725 mL) flour
1½ tsp (7 mL) baking powder
½ tsp (2 mL) salt

Cream shortening and sugar very well. It takes longer for maple sugar to work in. Add egg; beat well. Sift flour, baking powder, and salt together and add to batter. Shape dough into 2 in. (5 cm) cylinders; wrap in wax paper and chill. Slice ⅛ in. (0.25 cm) thick. Place on greased cookie sheets and bake 8-10 minutes in 400° oven.

PARKIN

1 cup (250 mL) butter	3 cups (750 mL) flour
1 cup (250 mL) molasses	2 tsp (10 mL) soda
1 cup (250 mL) brown sugar, not packed	2 medium (large) eggs
2 cups (500 mL) rolled oats	blanched almonds

Cream butter and sugar; add molasses and eggs. Sift the soda with the flour and add the rolled oats. Add dry ingredients to egg mixture. Place small balls on greased cookie sheet and put half an almond on top of each cookie. Bake 20 minutes in 350° oven.

SOFT MOLASSES COOKIES

1 cup (250 mL) molasses	4 tsp (20 mL) soda
1 cup (250 mL) brown sugar	4 cups (1 L) flour
1 cup (250 mL) butter	2 eggs
1 tsp (5 mL) salt	2 tsp (10 mL) ginger, or,
2 tsp (10 mL) cream of tartar	more if desired

Mix in order given; roll into balls and place on greased cookie sheet. Press with a fork and bake 10-12 minutes in 375° oven.

COCONUT MACAROONS

2 egg whites	¼ cup (60 mL) slivered almonds
1 cup (250 mL) granulated sugar	½ tsp (2 mL) almond flavouring
2 cups (500 mL) corn flakes	½ tsp (2 mL) salt
1 cup (250 mL) shredded coconut	

Toast almonds lightly on a cookie sheet under the broiler, stirring to toast on all sides. *Watch carefully.* Beat egg whites and salt stiff. Beat in half the sugar slowly; fold in remaining sugar carefully. Fold in remaining ingredients — corn flakes may be lightly crushed. Drop by spoonfuls ½ in. (1 cm) apart on greased sheet. Bake in 325° oven for 15 minutes. Let cool on cookie sheet, removing when cold.

BACHELOR BUTTONS

¼ cup (75 mL) butter
1⅓ cups (400 mL) sifted pastry flour
⅔ cup (200 mL) sugar
¼ tsp (1 mL) salt
½ tsp (3 mL) almond extract
1 large (2 small) eggs

Cut butter into flour as if for pastry. Beat eggs with half of sugar and mix with flour and butter. Add remainder of sugar, slowly, with salt and almond. Chill until firm. Roll bits of dough the size of a small walnut and place on greased cookie sheet. Bake at 375° for 12-15 minutes. Cool on rack. Note: Metric measures will make more cookies.

DUTCH DAINTIES

2 cups (500 mL) flour
2 tbsp (30 mL) sugar — fruit
  sugar if available
¼ tsp (1 mL) salt
1 tsp (5 mL) baking powder

¾ cup (185 mL) butter
1 beaten egg
2 tbsp (30 mL) milk
1 tsp (5 mL) vanilla
thick strawberry jam

Mix dry ingredients. Cut in butter finely and mix in egg and milk and vanilla. Mix well and chill. Roll thin and cut with 2½-3 in. (6-7.5 cm) round cutter. Put ½ tsp (3 mL) jam on one half; fold over and seal by pressing with fork. Place on a lightly greased cookie sheet. Bake 10-12 minutes in 375° oven. Cool on rack.

SUGAR COOKIES

2 cups (500 mL) flour
½ tsp (2 mL) salt
1 egg
1 tsp (5 mL) vanilla extract

1 stick (125 g) butter
1½ tsp (7 mL) baking powder
¾ cup (185 mL) granulated sugar
1 tbsp (15 mL) cream

Cream butter and sugar. Add beaten egg, cream, and vanilla. Mix well and add 1¾ cups (425 mL) of the flour, sifted with all the baking powder and salt. Add enough of the remaining flour until the dough is stiff enough to roll. Chill for at least 2 hours or overnight. Turn out on very lightly floured board and roll ⅛ in. (0.25 cm) thick. Cut into hearts or other shapes; place on ungreased baking sheets and sprinkle with sugar — pink sugar, if you can find any available to buy. Bake 8-10 minutes in 375° oven. Cool on rack.

OATMEAL COOKIES

2⅔ cups (665 mL) oatmeal
½ cup (125 mL) melted butter
1 cup (250 mL) brown sugar

Mix well. Pat onto greased cookie sheet. Bake 15 minutes in 350° oven. Cut while still hot.

OATMEAL COOKIES

2 cups (500 mL) rolled oats
2 cups (500 mL) flour
1 cup (250 mL) shortening or
  butter
½ cup (125 mL) brown sugar

1 cup (250 mL) white sugar
1 medium (large) egg, beaten
¼ cup (65 mL) water
½ tsp (2 mL) baking soda

Mix flour, oats, salt, and sugar. Rub in the fat and add the egg and water, with the soda mixed in. Roll thin on board well sprinkled with rolled oats. Cut in rounds and place on lightly greased cookie sheet. Bake 10-12 minutes in 400° oven.

APRICOT SQUARES

1 cup (250 mL) dried apricots	½ cup (125 mL) butter
½ cup (125 mL) water	⅔ cup (165 mL) sugar
quarter of a lemon	1½ cup (375 mL) flour
½ cup (125 mL) sugar	1 tsp (5 mL) baking powder
½ cup (125 mL) chopped walnuts	1 egg

Boil the apricots, water, and lemon, covered, for 10 minutes and stir in the sugar. Stir on heat till sugar is all melted. Put the mixture through the food chopper. Stir in the nuts and set aside. Cream butter and sugar; add egg; stir in flour and baking powder. This will make a stiff dough. Pat into a well-greased 9 x 9 in. (22 x 22 cm) cake tin. Spread the apricot puree on top and bake for 20 minutes in 400° oven. Cool and cut in squares.

MAPLE SPICE SQUARES

½ cup (125 mL) flour	½ tsp (2 mL) baking soda
½ cup (125 mL) sugar	¾ tsp (4 mL) cinnamon
¼ cup (65 mL) shortening, melted	¼ tsp (1 mL) cloves
¼ cup (65 mL) maple syrup	½ tsp (2 mL) salt
½ cup (125 mL) sour milk	½ cup (125 mL) finely chopped
1 egg	walnuts

Sift together flour, sugar, soda, salt, and spice. Beat egg; add milk, syrup, and shortening. Pour into flour; mix well. Pour into greased 11 x 8 in. (28 x 20 cm) pan and sprinkle with nuts. Bake in 325° oven for 35 minutes. Cool and cut in squares.

DATE SQUARES

Oatmeal Base:
1⅓ cups (400 mL) flour
pinch of baking soda
1¾ cups (525 mL) rolled oats
1 cup (300 mL) packed brown
sugar
¾ cup (225 mL) butter

Filling:
1 15 oz (500 g) package of dates
1 cup (250 mL) water
½ cup (125 mL) sugar
juice of 1 small (large) lemon

Mix filling ingredients in saucepan. Cook, stirring constantly until thickened.

Combine the dry ingredients for base. Rub in the butter. Divide this mixture in half and pat one half into a greased 9 in. (25 cm) pan. Spread with filling. Sprinkle other half of oatmeal mixture on top. Bake 45 minutes at 375°. Cool and cut into bars. Note: Metric measures will give more squares.

OATCAKES

2 cups (500 mL) medium oatmeal
— not rolled oats
1 cup (250 mL) flour
1 tsp (5 mL) salt
2 tsp (10 mL) baking powder

2 tsp (10 mL) sugar — optional
6 tbsp (95 mL) bacon fat, or,
margarine
¼ cup (65 mL) cold water

Sift flour, salt, and baking powder together. Add oatmeal and sugar. Work in the fat with the fingertips and mix water until the mixture is firm. Roll out on a surface dusted with oatmeal to a thickness of ¼ in. (0.5 cm). Cut into triangles and bake on lightly greased cookie sheet in 350° oven for 12-15 minutes. Serve with butter and cheese.

CHESS CAKES

1 cup (250 mL) flour
½ cup (125 mL) sugar
½ cup (125 mL) butter
2 eggs
grated lemon rind
1 tsp (5 mL) baking powder

3 egg whites
¼ tsp (1 mL) almond extract
½ cup (125 mL) blanched almonds, grated
6 tbsp (95 mL) sugar
raspberry jam

Cream butter; add first amount of sugar and beaten eggs. Add flour sifted with baking powder and lemon rind. Chill. Break off about 25 pieces and press each piece into a 2 in. (5 cm) muffin cup to form a shell. Chill while preparing filling.

Beat egg whites with almond extract until foamy; then gradually beat in sugar till mixture is stiff. Fold in grated almonds. Place 1 tsp (5 mL) raspberry jam in each shell and top with almond filling. Don't fill shells more than ⅔ full. Bake 30 minutes in 375° oven. Carefully remove from tins and cool on racks.

MRS. DWYER'S DOUGHNUTS

2 cups (500 mL) fluffy mashed potatoes
1¾ cups (435 mL) sugar — white or light brown
3 large (extra-large) beaten eggs
2 tbsp (30 mL) melted butter
5 cups (1250 mL) flour

4 tsp (20 mL) cream of tartar
2 tsp (10 mL) soda
1 cup (250 mL) milk
1 tsp (5 mL) salt
1 tsp heaping (6 mL) nutmeg
cinnamon sugar, or, icing sugar

Combine potatoes, sugar, eggs, and butter. Sift flour with soda, cream of tartar, salt, and nutmeg. Add to potatoes, alternately, with milk. Chill. Turn out on well floured board and roll out ½ in. (1 cm) thick. Cut with floured doughnut cutter. Fry doughnuts and holes in 360°F (182°C) fat. Turn once. Drain and roll in cinnamon sugar or sprinkle with icing sugar.

EASY DROP DOUGHNUTS

1 cup (250 mL) brown sugar
2 medium (large) eggs
½ cup (125 mL) milk
2 tbsp (30 mL) butter
3 cups (750 mL) flour

2 tsp (10 mL) cream of tartar
1 tsp (5 mL) soda
½ tsp (2 mL) salt
½ tsp (2 mL) nutmeg
icing sugar

Cream butter and sugar; add eggs, well beaten. Sift flour with cream of tartar, soda, salt, and nutmeg. Add to creamed mixture, alternately, with milk. Drop by spoonfuls into 360°F (182°C) fat. Fry until golden. Drain. Sift icing sugar over.

Cakes, Frostings, and Fillings

BIRTHDAY CAKE

1½ cups (375 mL) butter
2⅓ cups (580 mL) icing sugar
7 medium (extra-large) egg
  yolks

4½ cups (1125 mL) cake flour
2½ tsp (13 mL) baking powder
1¾ cups (435 mL) milk
1½ tsp (7 mL) vanilla extract

Cream butter and sugar. Beat egg yolks until very thick and pale — approximately 5 minutes at high speed on mixer — and add to creamed mixture. Sift flour before measuring; resift with salt and baking powder at least twice more. Add to creamed mixture, alternately with milk, folding in with rubber spatula or with the hand to give velvety texture. Add vanilla. Pour into three greased and floured 8 in. (20 cm) layer pans. Bake in 375° oven for 25-30 minutes until cake springs back when touched. Cool in pans for 10 minutes. Turn out and cool on wire cake rack. Frost and decorate with Decorator Frosting. Note: One or more layers may be tinted pink by the addition of food colouring.

DECORATOR FROSTING

1 cup (275 mL) butter
1 cup (275 mL) flour
1 cup (275 mL) water
2 lb (1 kg) icing sugar —
    approximately
1 tbsp vanilla extract, or, other
    flavour as desired

Cream butter until very light. Cream in flour. Add water and flavouring. Add sugar until desired consistency is reached. For frosting the cake you may use a thinner icing. Then, you may add additional sugar to make the icing thicker for putting decorations on the frosted cake.

WHITER-THAN-WHITE CAKE

¾ cup (225 mL) shortening
1½ cups (450 mL) sugar
3 cups (900 mL) sifted cake flour
4 tsp (25 mL) baking powder
½ tsp (3 mL) salt

1 cup (300 mL) milk
1 tsp (6 mL) almond extract
5 (7) egg whites
12 pastel-coloured jelly beans
1 package shredded coconut

Cream shortening and sugar till very fluffy. Sift flour, baking powder, and salt together and add, alternately with milk, to the shortening and sugar mixture. Beat egg whites stiff. Mix one fifth of them with batter, mixing well; fold the rest in carefully. Add almond. Pour into greased and floured 8 x 8 in. (22 x 22 cm) layer pans. Bake in 350° oven for 30 minutes. Remove from pans and cool. Frost and fill with Boiled Icing. Cover with shredded coconut and make nest shapes on cake. Put jelly bean eggs in nests. Note: The metric measures make a larger cake.

VALENTINE CAKE

1 cup (250 mL) butter
2 cups (500 mL) sugar
1 cup (250 mL) milk
3½ cups (875 mL) sifted cake flour
2 tsp (10 mL) baking powder

1 tsp (5 mL) vanilla extract
6 medium (large) egg whites
¼ tsp (1 mL) salt
¼ cup (50 mL) cut up candied
    cherries

Cream butter until it is almost white. Add sugar and cream and beat until very fluffy. Add egg whites and continue beating. Add the flour sifted with baking powder and salt. Add vanilla. Bake in two 8 in. (20 cm) greased and floured layer cake pans in 350° oven for 40 minutes. Cool on racks. Frost with Boiled Icing.

BOILED ICING

1½ cups (375 mL) sugar
½ cup (125 mL) water
1½ tsp (8 mL) vinegar
3 medium (large) egg whites
1 tsp (5 mL) vanilla extract
few grains of salt

Boil sugar, water, and vinegar, without stirring, to 238°F (115°C) or until it spins a thread. Meantime, beat egg whites with salt till stiff, and gradually pour in syrup, beating constantly until icing keeps its shape. Add vanilla. This is the basic Boiled Icing; however, if desired, for Valentine Cake fold in 1 cup (250 mL) of halved candied cherries after adding vanilla.

CHOCOLATE CAKE

¾ cup (225 mL) butter
1¾ cup (525 mL) firmly packed
  brown sugar
1 medium (extra-large) egg
3 large (extra-large) egg yolks
4 squares (150 g) unsweetened
  chocolate

2¼ cups (675 mL) flour
1½ tsp (10 mL) baking soda
¼ tsp (1 mL) salt
1½ cups (450 mL) light cream
1½ tsp (10 mL) vanilla extract

Cream together butter and sugar. Add egg; beat well. Add the egg yolks one at a time, beating after each one. Melt chocolate and add. Sift together flour and baking soda; add, alternately with cream, to butter mixture. Add vanilla. Pour into two greased and floured 9 in. (25 cm) layer pans. Bake 40 minutes in 350° oven. Cool 5 minutes. Remove from pans and cool on rack. Frost. Note: The metric measures will yield a larger cake.

CHOCOLATE FROSTING

4 squares unsweetened chocolate
1 13 oz (365 mL) can sweetened
condensed milk
1 tbsp (15 mL) water
½ tsp (2 mL) vanilla extract
½ tsp (2 mL) almond extract, or, brandy,
or, rum

Melt chocolate in double boiler; add milk; cook 5 minutes, stirring constantly, until thickened. Add water and flavouring.

BUTTER CAKE

1 cup (250 mL) butter
1½ cups (375 mL) white sugar
5 medium (large) eggs
1 cup (250 mL) milk

2 tsp (10 mL) cream of tartar
1 tsp (5 mL) soda
3½ cups (875 mL) flour

Cream butter till very light; add sugar gradually while creaming till fluffy. Beat eggs well and add milk. Sift soda and cream of tartar with flour. Add dry ingredients and liquid, alternately, to creamed mixture. Pour into three greased and floured 9 in. (22 cm) layer pans. Bake in 375° oven for 25-30 minutes. Fill and frost with Lemon Filling and Daffodil Frosting.

LEMON FILLING

¼ cup (75 mL) sugar
3 tbsp (55 mL) flour
½ tsp (2 mL) salt
½ cup (150 mL) water
2 tbsp (35 mL) lemon juice

½ tsp (2 mL) grated lemon rind
1 tbsp (20 mL) butter
⅓ cup (100 mL) chopped nuts
1 cup (300 mL) chopped dates

Mix sugar, flour, and salt. Slowly add water, stirring constantly to avoid lumps. Cook in top of double boiler until mixture is thick. Add butter; when melted, add lemon juice and rind and fold in dates and nuts.

DAFFODIL FROSTING

6 tbsp (100 mL) butter
2 cups (535 mL) icing sugar
3 tbsp (50 mL) orange juice
pinch of salt
½ tsp (1 mL) lemon rind

5-6 drops yellow colouring
2-3 drops green colouring
2 tbsp (30 mL) icing sugar
small amount milk

Cream butter; add some of the sugar until the mixture is very stiff; then beat in orange juice, lemon rind, and salt. Add rest of the 2 cups (535 mL) of sugar until frosting is of good consistency. Reserve about ½ cup (130 mL) icing and add yellow color to the rest. Add green to the ½ cup (130 mL) of icing. Mix the 2 tbsp (30 mL) icing sugar with enough milk to make stiff white icing. Frost cake with yellow icing. Use green to make stems and leaves all around edge of cake and place dots of white icing on stems to represent snow drops. Swirl yellow icing on top in daffodil design.

WASHINGTON PIE

1 cup (225 mL) cake flour
1 tsp (5 mL) baking powder
pinch of salt
3 eggs

1 cup (225 mL) sugar
2 tsp (10 mL) lemon juice
6 tbsp (85 mL) milk
1 tsp (5 mL) butter

Sift together the flour, baking powder, and salt. Beat the eggs until they are very light and have doubled in volume. Gradually add sugar, beating all the while. Add lemon juice. Fold in the flour mixture in four portions. Heat the milk and butter and stir quickly into batter. Pour into 9 in. (25 cm) ungreased tube pan. Bake in 350° oven for 45 minutes. Invert pan on rack for 1 hour. Loosen cake and remove from pan. Cut cake in half crosswise and fill with Fruit Filling and Cream Topping.

FRUIT FILLING AND CREAM TOPPING

½ pt (200 mL) whipping cream
2 tbsp (30 mL) confectioners' sugar
½ tsp (2 mL) vanilla extract
sliced bananas, or, peaches, or,
strawberries, sweetened

Whip the cream, adding the sugar and vanilla. Fold in the fruit, and fill and frost cake layers to make Washington Pie.

TOMATO SOUP CAKE

¼ cup (60 mL) shortening
⅞ cup (210 mL) white sugar
2 medium (large) eggs
1½ cups (360 mL) sifted pastry
    flour
¼ tsp (1 mL) soda

1 tsp (5 mL) baking powder
1 tsp (5 mL) cinnamon
⅔ cup (160 mL) tomato soup,
    undiluted
¾ cup (180 mL) raisins

Cream shortening and sugar. Add eggs and beat well. Sift the flour with soda, baking powder, and spice and add to creamed mixture, alternately with the soup straight from the can. Fold in the raisins and pour batter into a greased and floured 8 x 8 in. (20 x 20 cm) pan; bake 45 minutes in 350° oven.

SELF-ICED CAKE

¼ cup (65 mL) butter
½ cup (125 mL) sugar
1 cup (250 mL) flour
¼ cup (65 mL) milk

1 tsp (5 mL) baking powder
½ tsp (10 mL) vanilla
¼ tsp (2 mL) salt
3 medium (large) egg yolks

Cream butter and sugar. Add egg yolks and beat well. Sift flour with baking powder and salt and add to creamed mixture, alternately with the milk. Add vanilla. Place in greased 8 x 8 in. (20 x 20 cm) pan and put this meringue on top of the raw cake.

3 egg whites
½ cup (125 mL) white or brown sugar
slivered almonds

Beat egg whites till stiff and gradually beat in sugar. Spread on cake and sprinkle with almonds. Bake cake in 350° oven for 30-35 minutes.

MAPLE UPSIDE-DOWN CAKE

¼ cup (65 mL) butter
1 cup (250 mL) grated maple sugar
2 medium (large) eggs
⅔ cup (165 mL) sugar
¼ cup (60 mL) hot water

⅓ cup (80 mL) pastry flour
¾ tsp (4 mL) baking powder
¼ tsp (1 mL) salt
⅓ tsp (2 mL) vanilla extract
½ cup (125 mL) halved pecans, or, walnuts

Melt butter in 8 in. (20 cm) pan. Sprinkle maple sugar over and add nut meats upside down. Whip eggs with sugar; add water. Sift flour with baking powder and salt. Fold into egg mixture and add vanilla. Pour over mixture already in pan. Before baking, lift the pan full of cake batter about 1 in. (2.5 cm) into the air and then let it drop back sharply onto the counter. Repeat two or three times, in order to dislodge air bubbles from the bottom of the cake and bring them to the surface. This gives the cake a better texture. Then, bake in 300° oven for 40 minutes. Turn upside down on serving dish. Serve warm with whipped cream.

MARBLE CAKE

1 cup (250 mL) shortening
2 cups (500 mL) sugar
4 large (extra-large) eggs
3 cups (750 mL) cake flour
4 tsp (21 mL) baking powder
¾ tsp (4 mL) salt
1 cup (250 mL) milk
1 tsp (5 mL) vanilla extract

1½ oz (40 g) unsweetened chocolate
pinch of baking soda
2 tbsp (30 mL) boiling water
¼ tsp (1 mL) almond extract
2 tbsp (30 mL) raspberry jelly, or, strawberry jelly, or, syrup from strawberry preserves

Cream shortening and sugar. Add eggs, one at a time, beating well after each. Sift flour with baking powder and salt. Add, alternating with milk, to creamed mixture. Add vanilla. Melt chocolate and add water and soda to it. Melt the jelly and add a little water, enough to keep it runny. Divide batter in three and add chocolate to one third and jelly to another. Spoon each color alternately into greased 9 in. (22 cm) tube pan. Cut through twice in opposite directions to swirl colours. Bake 1¼ hours in 350° oven. Cool 10 minutes in pan on rack. Turn out. Cool and frost with thin layer of melted Fondant.

GREAT GRANDMOTHER'S SALT PORK CHRISTMAS CAKE

½ lb (250 g) fat salt pork —
  fat only, without the lean
1½ cups (375 mL) sugar
1½ cups (375 mL) molasses
3 large (extra-large) eggs
1 cup (250 mL) milk
1 cup (250 mL) flour

1 tsp (5 mL) soda
1 nutmeg, grated
1 tsp (5 mL) cinnamon
½ tsp (2 mL) cloves
¾ tsp (3 mL) allspice
1 lb (500 g) seeded raisins
½ lb (250 g) candied citron

Sift flour with spices. Set aside ½ cup (125 mL). Cut up raisins, combine with citron and dredge with the ½ cup (125 mL) of flour mixture. Cut the pork fat into small pieces and cream as you would butter; when well creamed, add sugar, molasses, and eggs. Add soda to remaining flour-spice mixture and add to batter, alternately with milk. Pour over fruit mixture and combine thoroughly. Pour into 8 in. (20 cm) square or round, 3 in. (7 cm) deep cake tin, lined with greased, heavy, brown paper. Bake 4 hours in 275° oven, or till cake tests done.

WEDDING CAKES: 1. GROOM'S CAKE

1 lb (450 g) all purpose flour
1¼ lb (560 g) brown sugar
1 lb (450 g) butter
1 dozen eggs
1 tbsp (15 mL) cinnamon
½ tbsp (7 mL) allspice
½ tbsp (7 mL) nutmeg
8 oz (225 g) strawberry jam
2 lb (900 g) chopped dates
2 lb (900 g) glacé cherries

4 oz (110 g) chopped, blanched
   almonds
2 lb (900 g) seedless raisins
2 lb (900 g) seeded raisins,
   chopped
1 lb (450 g) currants
½ lb (225 g) mixed peel
1 cup (225 mL) brandy
1 14 oz (398 mL) can pineapple
   chunks, drained

The Groom's Cake is a dark fruitcake.

Combine all the fruit and nuts with 2 cups (450 mL) of flour. Cream the butter and sugar till fluffy. Add eggs, 1 at a time beating well. Add strawberry jam and brandy. Mix spices with remaining flour and mix in. Pour batter over prepared fruit and mix very well. Line two 11 x 4½ in. (28 x 11.5 cm) or two 8 in. (20 cm) square pans with greased, heavy, brown paper and pour batter in. Let stand overnight and bake 4 hours in 250° oven. Let cool in pans; remove; put the two cakes together, side by side, and ice as one large sheet. Cover with ¼ in. (0.5 cm) layer of Almond Paste and frost with Royal Icing.

ALMOND PASTE

1 lb (500 g) blanched almonds
1 lb (500 g) icing sugar
2 large (extra-large) eggs

Grind almonds in blender or food processor; add enough sugar to take up the oil that comes out of the almonds. After all the almonds have been ground, run them through again. Add the rest of sugar and beaten eggs and mix well. Dust board with powdered sugar and knead well till smooth. Roll out ¼ in. (0.5) thick and cut to fit cakes.

ROYAL ICING

2 egg whites
1 lb (500 g) icing sugar
2 tbsp (30 mL) lemon juice

Beat egg whites lightly and add enough sugar to make icing that will hold shape. Blend in lemon juice to get desired consistency. Spread over Almond Paste on cake and let harden. Decorate.

WEDDING CAKES: 2. BRIDE'S CAKE

1½ lb (725 mL) butter
5¼ cups (1260 mL) all purpose
   flour
⅜ tsp (2 mL) soda
¾ tsp (3 mL) mace
4½ tbsp (65 mL) lemon juice

4½ cups (1075 mL) sugar
1½ tbsp (25 mL) vanilla
15 eggs, separated
⅜ tsp (2 mL) salt
1½ tsp (7 mL) cream of tartar

The Bride's Cake is a three-tier white cake.

Prepare three round tube pans, 10 in. (25 cm), 8 in. (20 cm), and 5 in. (12 cm) in diameter. If tube pans are not available, straight-sided glass tumblers may be greased and floured and placed in the centre of round pans of the correct diameter. Small stones can be used to weight the tumblers. Grease pans well and dust with flour. Mix this cake with the hands. Sift flour, soda, mace, and half of the sugar into a large bowl. Rub in the butter with the hands. Add lemon juice and vanilla to the egg yolks and add these, a few at a time to the flour and butter mixture mixing with the hand. Whip the egg whites in a large metal or china bowl with the salt and cream of tartar until stiff. Gradually beat in the other half of the sugar till the whites are very stiff and glossy. Add the whites to the cake in four portions, folding in gently with the hands until no white lumps are visible. Spoon into prepared pans and bake in preheated 300° oven 2½ hours for 10 in. (25 cm) pan, 2¼ hours for 8 in. (20 cm) pan, and 1½ hours for 5 in. (12 cm) pan. Cakes are done when they shrink from the sides of pans. Remove small cake from oven and let stand in pan on rack for 1 hour before turning out. When 8 in. (20 cm) cake is done turn off oven and let stand for ½ hour more; remove it and 15 minutes later take out 10 in. (25 cm) cake. Let these cakes stand on rack for ½ hour and then turn out on rack. Let cakes cool overnight before frosting. If the cake tiers are separated by pillars, the holes left by the tube pans may be covered by rounds of cardboard before they are iced. Use Decorator Frosting and decorate with candied roses or fresh flowers.

CRYSTALLIZED ROSE PETALS

wild roses
superfine fruit sugar
egg white

Early in the morning, pick freshly opened wild roses. Separate the petals and brush each one with a paint brush dipped in lightly beaten egg white. Cover a cookie sheet with the sugar and lay the petals on it. Sprinkle more sugar over the petals. Set sheets in a very warm, very dry place for 2 or 3 days. To decorate cake, reform flowers from single petals. If petals turn brown or shrivel, insufficient sugar was used or place was not dry enough. Violets may be candied in the same way but do not keep well. To keep, violets should be candied in syrup.

CANDIED VIOLETS

1 lb (500 g) sugar
1½ cups (425 mL) water
4 cups (1 L) violets

Nip the stems off violets. Cook sugar in water to 238°F (115°C). Cool. Pour sugar syrup into a cake pan to a depth of 1 in. (2.5 cm) put a cake rack in the syrup and spread the violets on it submerging them. Cover the pan with a wet cloth and let stand 6 hours. Add more syrup to cover flowers again. Put cloth over pan again and let stand overnight. Next day remove flowers, drain and dry. Roll dried flowers in a little dry sugar.

MAPLE ICING

½ lb (225 g) grated maple sugar
2 unbeaten egg whites
5 tbsp (70 mL) cold water
1 tbsp (15 mL) corn syrup

Place in upper part of double boiler over rapidly boiling water and beat with electric mixer until frosting stands in peaks — 8-10 minutes.

BUTTER CREAM ICING

½ cup (125 mL) sugar
pinch of cream of tartar
2 tbsp (30 mL) water
2 large (extra-large) egg yolks
½ cup (125 mL) butter, softened
1 tsp (5 mL) vanilla extract

Combine water, sugar, and cream of tartar in a heavy saucepan. Stir till sugar dissolves; then boil, without stirring, to 244°F (118°C) or till it spins a thread. Cool syrup for about a minute while beating egg yolks till thick; then slowly pour syrup into yolks. When all syrup is added, beat in the butter a little at a time. Add vanilla or other flavouring — mint, coffee, lemon, brandy or 1 oz (28 g) of chocolate. Continue beating till frosting is cool. Chill to proper consistency for spreading. Store frosting, and cakes frosted with it, in a cool place.

Jams, Jellies, and Pickles

DAMSON AND MARROW JAM

3 lb (1.5 kg) damson plums
3 lb (1.5 kg) vegetable marrow
2 cups (500 mL) water
sugar

Peel and seed the marrow. Chop coarsely and simmer with 1 cup (250 mL) water until tender. Cut the damsons in half; remove pits and simmer with 1 cup (250 mL) of water until very tender. Rub damsons through a sieve, or food mill, and combine with cooked, drained marrow. Weigh and combine with an equal weight of sugar. Heat gently until sugar is dissolved and then boil rapidly until thick. Ladle into sterilized glasses and seal.

BLUEBERRY JAM

1½ qt (1.5 L) blueberries
1 lemon
5 cups (1125 mL) sugar

Wash blueberries; place in preserving kettle; mash and add lemon juice. Add sugar, stir, and bring to a boil. Simmer till thickened. Let stand 15 minutes; skim, stir, and pour into sterilized glasses. Seal.

BLACK CURRANT JAM

4 cups (1 L) black currants
3¼ lb (1.5 kg) sugar

Top and tail the currants. Crush and mix with sugar in preserving kettle. Bring to a boil and cook 10-15 minutes or until thick. Let stand 15 minutes; skim, stir, and pour into sterilized glasses. Seal.

GOOSEBERRY JAM

1 qt (1 L) gooseberries
1 large orange
half a lemon
3 cups (600 mL) sugar

Top and tail gooseberries. Wash. Grate rind of lemon and orange. Remove membrane and chop pulp of lemon and orange. Crush gooseberries in preserving kettle; add rind and pulp of orange and lemon. Stir in sugar and bring to boil. Simmer, stirring, until thick. Pour in sterilized glasses and seal.

RASPBERRY JAM

2 lb (1 kg) fresh, hulled raspberries
2 lb (1 kg) sugar

Crush berries and rub half of them through a sieve to remove some seeds. Discard the seeds. Put berries in preserving kettle and bring to the boil. Add sugar; boil slowly, stirring until thick. Pour into hot, sterilized jars.

RHUBARB-STRAWBERRY JAM

1 cup (250 mL) diced rhubarb
1 cup (250 mL) water
4 cups (1000 mL) strawberries, washed and hulled
3 cups (750 mL) sugar

Cook rhubarb with water till soft. Add strawberries. Simmer 10 minutes. Add sugar. Boil until thick. Skim, and bottle in sterilized jars.

GRAPE JELLY

    3 qt (3 L) concord grapes
    ½ cup (125 mL) water
    7 cups (1600 mL) sugar
    1 package pectin

Wash and stem grapes, discarding green, moldy or mushy fruit. Put in kettle with water; mash; bring to a boil and simmer, covered, 10 minutes. Pour into jelly bag and let drip, undisturbed. Measure 4 cups (1 L) of juice; add pectin and bring to boil. Dump in sugar all at once and bring to boil. Boil until two drops hang side by side from a spoon. Skim and pour into sterilized glasses. Seal. If grape jelly is stored too long it will develop crystals due to the tartaric acid in the grape skins.

MINT JELLY

    1½ cups (375 mL) firmly packed mint leaves
    3¼ cups (800 mL) boiling water
    4 cups (1000 mL) sugar
    1 package pectin
    few drops of green coloring
    6 perfect mint leaves

Coarsely chop the mint leaves and pour the boiling water over them. Stir well and let stand 15 minutes. Strain and measure out 3 cups (750 mL) of mint tea; add green colour. Bring to a boil with the pectin; when liquid is boiling hard, dump in all the sugar. Bring back to the boil and boil hard until you see two drops, side by side, hanging from the edge of the spoon. Pour into six sterile jelly glasses and float 1 leaf in each. Seal with paraffin if the jelly is to be kept.

RASPBERRY JELLY

    about 5 qt (5 L) ripe raspberries
    5½ cups (1 kg) sugar
    1 package pectin

Mash the berries thoroughly. Place in jelly bag and let drip. For beautiful clear jelly do not squeeze bag — do not even *touch* it. Measure 4 cups (900 mL) juice and bring to a boil with the pectin. Dump in all the sugar; bring back to a hard boil, stirring, and boil 1 minute or until two drops hang, side by side, on the edge of the spoon. Skim and pour into nine or ten sterilized jelly glasses. Seal with paraffin. Note: It is important to use pectin in making raspberry jelly. These fruits have little pectin and if you try to boil syrup to a "jelly" you will get a stringy, treacly consistency and the flavour will be far too strong.

RED CURRANT JELLY

3 qt (3 L) red currants
2 cups (500 mL) water
about 4 cups (1 L) sugar

Pick over the currants, removing stems and leaves. Do not discard the white, unripe fruits as they contain more pectin. Wash and place currants in kettle; add water; bring to a boil; reduce heat and simmer covered 20 minutes. Mash the fruit and pour into a jelly bag. Let drip undisturbed. Measure out 3 cups (1 L) juice and add an equal volume of sugar. Bring to a boil and boil hard until two drops hang side by side on a spoon. Remove from heat; skim and ladle into sterilized glasses. Seal.
Black Currant Jelly may be made in the same manner only adding 1 extra cup (250 mL) of water.

ROWANBERRY JELLY

3 lb (1.5 kg) rowanberries
1 lb (0.5 kg) sweet crab apples
2 lb (1 kg) sugar — approximately

Gather rowanberries after the first frost. Wash them well and remove all stalks. Stem the crab apples and cut off blossom end with a potato peeler. Chop apples coarsely. Combine apples and rowans in preserving kettle; add water to cover and simmer 45 minutes. Pour into jelly bag and let drip undisturbed. Measure juice and add 2 lb of sugar (900 kg) to every qt (1250 mL) of juice. Place over high heat and boil quickly until two drops hang, side by side, on the edge of spoon. Skim, and pour into sterilized jars. This jelly is very tart.

CHOKECHERRY JELLY

4 qt (4 L) slightly underripe chokecherries
1 package pectin
4 cups (1000 mL) sugar

Wash and stem the chokecherries. The bulk of the fruits should be red rather than fully ripe black. If too great a proportion of black fruit is used, the jelly will be cloudy but will taste fine. Place fruit in preserving kettle and cover with water. Bring to a boil and simmer, covered, ½ hour. Mash fruit well. Pour into jelly bag and let drip, undisturbed. Measure 4 cups (1000 mL) juice. Add pectin and bring to a boil. Add sugar and boil hard until two drops hang, side by side, on spoon. Skim, and pour into sterilized jars. Seal.

CRAB APPLE JELLY

5 lb (2.5 kg) tart crab apples
4 lb (2 kg) sugar
5 cups (1250 mL) water

Be sure that many of the apples are bright red. Remove stems and blossom ends. Chop coarsely. Add water to apples and simmer, covered, for 15 minutes. Mash; pour into jelly bag and let drip undisturbed. Measure out 7 cups (1750 mL) of juice. Add sugar and boil hard until two drops hang, side by side, on the spoon. Skim; pour into sterilized jelly glasses and seal.

BLACKBERRY JELLY

2 qt (2 L) blackberries, including a
  few underripe ones
2 cups (500 mL) water
5 cups (1025 mL) sugar
1 package pectin

Mix berries with water; bring to boil and simmer 25 minutes. Mash berries; place in jelly bag and let drain overnight. Collect juice. Measure out 3½ cups (875 mL) of juice. Add sugar and bring to a full rolling boil. Stir in pectin and continue boiling until two drops of jelly hang, side by side, on the spoon. Remove from heat; skim, and pour into sterilized jelly glasses. Cover and store.

ORANGE MARMALADE

4 sweet oranges
2 lemons
12 cups (2.75 L) water
6 lb (2.75 kg) sugar

Skin the fruit, removing some pith. Cut up the skin and discard the pith. Chop pulp and add to skin. Remove seeds. Add water and let stand 24 hours. Boil 1 hour. Add sugar; boil slowly until it jells — usually about 1 more hour. Bottle and paraffin.

SCOTCH MARMALADE

2 bitter — Seville — oranges
6 sweet oranges
lemons
sugar

Peel fruit; seed; chop pulp. Put seeds in cheesecloth bag. Shred the peel. To the pulp, add water to cover and bring to boil, pressing pulp well then rubbing through sieve, holding back white membrane. Add peel and measure. To each 4 cups (1 L) of juice add 1 lb (0.5 kg) of sugar and the juice and rind of 1 lemon for every 4 lb (2 kg) of oranges. Add sugar and lemon to juice and peel; boil with seed bag until mixture gels. Remove seed bag; bottle.

GINGER AND MARROW MARMALADE

3 lb (1.5 kg) diced vegetable marrow
3 lb (1.5 kg) sugar
3 lemons
½ lb (225 g) candied ginger, cut fine
1 tsp (5 mL) ground ginger

Peel and seed marrows and dice into ¼ in. (0.5 cm) cubes. Weigh out 3 lb (1.5 kg) and combine with equal weight of sugar. Cover and leave overnight; by morning, liquid will have drained out of marrow. Place everything in kettle; stir; add the lemon peel, grated, the lemon juice, the ground ginger, and the crystallized ginger. Heat gently, stirring to dissolve sugar, and simmer until the syrup is thick. This preserve does not jell so it is important to cook it until it is quite thick.

BOTTLED PEACHES

1 4 qt (4 L) basket of peaches, firm and ripe
2¼ cups (575 mL) sugar
3 cups (750 mL) water

Boil a large kettle of water and drop peaches in, a few at a time. Let stand 1 minute; then plunge peaches into cold water. Slip off skins, halve the fruit; remove pits. Cover with hot syrup, made by boiling sugar with 3 cups (1275 mL) water for 5 minutes. Simmer for 5-10 minutes until fruit is tender but not soft. Crack one or two pits and simmer along with the fruit for stronger flavour. Pack the hot fruit into hot mason jars. Add hot syrup to within ½ in. (1 cm) of the top. Put lids on but do not screw down hard. Leave about one-quarter turn. Place jars on rack in deep kettle and cover with boiling water. When water is boiling vigorously start counting time. Process for 15 minutes. Remove from water and screw lids tightly.

CHERRY PRESERVES

2 lb (1 kg) pitted sour red cherries, halved
3 lb (1.5 kg) sugar
2 cups (500 mL) red currants — optional

Mash the currants and add to the cherries in preserving kettle. Add the sugar and mix well. Bring to the boil slowly, stirring. Increase heat and boil hard for 10 minutes stirring and skimming. Let cool; stir to prevent floating fruit, bottle and seal. If red currants are omitted there will be less pectin and the syrup will be runnier.

BETTY MUNRO'S BEST STRAWBERRY PRESERVES

2 qt (2 L) strawberries
5 cups (1125 mL) sugar

Wash berries in cold water and then hull them. Place berries in a white or light coloured bowl and pour boiling water over them. As soon as water starts to get pink, drain the berries. Place in preserving kettle and bring to a boil. Boil 3 minutes. Add 2 cups (450 mL) sugar and boil 3 minutes more. Add 3 cups (675 mL) sugar and boil 3 minutes more. Take off the heat but let stand till cold before bottling. This keeps the colour and juice in the berries and makes the preserves look and taste superb.

MUSTARD PICKLES

7 large cucumbers
1 small head cauliflower
2 cups (500 mL) pearl onions
coarse salt
3 cups (750 mL) vinegar
1 cup (250 mL) water
2½ cups (625 mL) white sugar

½ cup (125 mL) flour
3 tbsp (45 mL) dry mustard
1 tbsp (15 mL) turmeric
1 tsp (5 mL) ginger
1 tsp (5 mL) whole cloves
salt to taste

Separate cauliflower into flowerettes. Cut cucumbers into quarters, lengthwise and cut crosswise into ¾ in. (2 cm) pieces. Peel onions — this is easy to do if you use the following method: cut a small cross in the bottom and then cover with boiling water; let stand and the skins slip off. Sprinkle cucumbers and onions with coarse salt and let stand 2 hours. Make the sauce by combining dry ingredients and mixing with water to make a paste. Boil vinegar and add paste to it stirring constantly. Taste for seasoning and add salt. Cook 5 minutes. Add drained, rinsed cucumbers, onions, and cauliflower and cook 10 minutes more. Pack in sterilized jars and seal.

PICKLED BEETS

4 cups (1 L) baby beets
1 cup (250 mL) vinegar
2 cups (500 mL) brown sugar
6 cloves

Cook the beets in boiling, salted water till tender. Slip off the skins and pack the beets into sterilized jars. Bring vinegar, sugar, and cloves to a boil; cook 3 minutes and pour over beets, being sure there is at least 1 clove in each jar. Seal.

ALEX MacBAIN'S CUCUMBER PICKLES

1 gal (4.5 L) cider vinegar
1 cup (250 mL) salt
1 cup (250 mL) dry mustard
1 cup (250 mL) brown sugar
pinch of alum
1 4 qt (4 L) basket of pickling cucumbers

Pack washed cucumbers into a large crock. Combine all other ingredients and pour over, making sure cucumbers are covered completely. These may be kept all winter. To use as needed, soak and cut up.

BREAD AND BUTTER PICKLES

1 qt (1 L) sliced cucumbers
coarse salt
1 large onion, sliced
1 cup (250 mL) brown sugar

1 tsp (5 mL) white mustard seed
1½ tsp (7 mL) pepper
2 tsp (10 mL) celery seed
vinegar

Slice the cucumbers ¼ in. (0.5 cm) thick. Sprinkle with coarse salt and let stand overnight. Next morning, drain the cucumbers and reserve in a basin. Combine sugar, mustard, pepper, and celery seed with a little vinegar and add. Continue to pour in vinegar until you can see it rising around the cucumbers. It should not quite cover them. Drain this measured amount of vinegar solution into a large kettle and bring to a boil. Add the cucumbers and the sliced onion and boil 5 minutes. Pack into sterilized jars and seal.

BRINE-PICKLED CUCUMBERS

cucumbers
coarse salt
water

Wash whole cucumbers well and pack them into a big crock until the crock is filled to within a few inches (centimetres) of the top. Add a layer of grape or beet leaves, about 1 in. (2.5 cm) thick. If any spoilage should occur on surface this will protect the cucumbers underneath. Make a brine with coarse salt, concentrated enough to float a potato, and pour into the crock until all the materials are covered. Place a clean board on top, weighted with a stone — do not use a metal weight. Let stand 24 hours; then put the lid on the crock to make it air tight, and allow to ferment. In a warm place, this will take about a week; in a cool cellar, 3 weeks to 1 month will be necessary for complete fermentation. Leave in crock and use as needed; or bottle. Dill pickles may be made by placing layers of dill between the cucumbers and adding a handful of mixed pickling spice.

PICKLED ONIONS

2 qt (2 L) small white onions
4½ cups (1 L) coarse salt
6 qt (6 L plus 725 mL) boiling
   water
cloves

strips of red pepper
bits of bay leaf
2 qt (2 L) white vinegar
½ cup (125 mL) white sugar

Peel onions. Combine 2 qt (2 L) boiling water with 1½ cups (375 mL) of salt. Pour over onions in a crock and let stand 2 days. Drain. Make the same amount of brine again; pour over onions and let stand 2 more days. Drain. Make third lot of brine; add onions and boil 3 minutes. Drain. Put onion in jars garnishing with a few cloves, bits of pepper, and bay leaf. Fill jars to overflowing with hot vinegar in which sugar is dissolved. Cover while hot.

CHILI SAUCE

20 ripe tomatoes
4 onions
4 green peppers
4 cups (1 L) vinegar

2 tbsp (30 mL) salt
2 cups (500 mL) brown sugar
1 tsp (5 mL) mixed spices
¼ tsp (1 mL) cayenne pepper

Put tomatoes, onions, and green peppers through the coarse blade of food chopper. Add rest of ingredients and simmer 2 hours. Put in sterilized jars and seal.

CHOW

12 lb (5.5 kg) green tomatoes
6 large onions, peeled
1 cup (225 mL) coarse salt
1 qt (1125 mL) white vinegar
4 lb (1800 g) white sugar

¼ cup (65 mL) pickling spice in gauze bag
1 small red pepper, seeded and cut in small chips

Wash tomatoes and onions. Cube tomatoes — it is important that no reddish pieces are included. Put in heavy earthenware bowl. Slice onions thinly and add to tomatoes. Sprinkle salt all over. Cover with a plate and weight down with a stone. Leave overnight. Next day, drain; pour boiling water to cover; drain again. Place in large preserving kettle; add remaining ingredients. Bring to a boil and cook until tender. Pack in sterilized jars. Seal.

Index